W9-CTF-644

MONEY 101

MONEY 101

*Every Canadian's Guide
to Personal Finance*

Ellen Roseman

Copyright © 2002 by Ellen Roseman

All rights reserved. No part of this work covered by the copyright herein may be reproduced or used in any form or by any means—graphic, electronic or mechanical—without the prior written permission of the publisher. Any request for photocopying, recording, taping or information storage and retrieval systems of any part of this book shall be directed in writing to CANCOPY, 1 Yonge Street, Suite 1900, Toronto, Ontario, M5E 1E5.

Care has been taken to trace ownership of copyright material contained in this book. The publishers will gladly receive any information that will enable them to rectify any reference or credit line in subsequent editions.

This publication contains opinions and ideas of the author. They are not presented to provide a basis of action for any particular circumstances without consideration by a competent professional. The author and publisher expressly disclaim any liability, loss, or risk, personal or otherwise, which is incurred as a consequence, direct or indirect, of the use or application of the contents of this book.

National Library of Canada Cataloguing in Publication

Roseman, Ellen, 1947-
    Money 101 : every Canadian's guide to personal finance / Ellen Roseman.

Includes index.
ISBN 0-470-83236-3

    1. Finance, Personal--Canada. I. Title. II. Title: Money one hundred one.

HG179.R674 2002   332.024'00971   C2002-905390-0

Production Credits
Cover & interior text design: Interrobang Graphic
    Design Inc.
Printer: Tri-Graphic Printing Ltd.
Printed in Canada
10 9 8 7 6 5 4 3 2 1

John Wiley & Sons Canada, Ltd
22 Worcester Road
Etobicoke, Ontario
M9W 1L1

Contents

Contents

Contents

Contents

Introduction

You want to make your money go further and set a little aside for savings. But your eyes glaze over when you hear about the dividend tax credit, dollar-cost averaging or derivatives.

This book is for you.

Money 101 is about mastering personal finance without pain. Think of it as a slow jog along the highway from idiocy to literacy.

My aim is to make the information understandable to everyone. This means breaking each topic into bite-sized chunks and keeping the writing simple (but not condescending), lively and opinionated.

The goal is to demystify money, to defeat the impression that only a math whiz can grasp the ins and outs of the subject. That's why there are no graphs or charts in these pages.

I want you to sense the urgency of getting a handle on your finances, even if you're uncomfortable with numbers and never follow the business news.

Why is it so important for everyone to go through a basic course in financial literacy?

- The income of the average Canadian family is stagnant. Only a few are doing better than inflation. Most households struggle to maintain their standard of living by working more, spending less or taking on higher levels of debt.

- The education system does a lousy job of teaching money skills. Teenagers graduate from high school knowing little about credit cards, car loans and chequing accounts—things they will soon confront.

- Many of us learn about money through trial and error, a costly way to find our bearings. We sign one-sided contracts without getting advice. Only then, after we have a problem, do we read the fine print.

As a consumer reporter for 30 years, I always keep the consumer's interest in mind. What is the danger, the drawback, the downside, to a deal? Where are the hidden traps to watch out for? What's not being said?

I hope to help readers avoid making expensive money mistakes. You can cover the cost of this book if you find just one or two tips that will improve your financial decision-making. But I'm sure you'll find more than that.

Here's our itinerary, the road map for the trip we're taking together in these pages.

We'll start by looking at how you spend your money and how you can save for the future. Then we'll move on to borrowing money for mortgages, car loans and credit cards. This is all part of shoring up your financial foundation.

Our next step is to look at retirement planning. Don't think this is a subject you can put off till you're over 40. You can start saving in an RRSP when you're a teenager and withdraw the money for a first home or an educational program. Or you can devote yourself to paying off your debts before you quit work. Some people retire early and then come back to work, while others never leave. But all of us have to think about it and make some plans.

After that, we'll look at investments. You need to understand the difference between stocks and bonds and know what fits within your comfort zone for risk. Do you have the temperament to be a successful investor? Or will you sleep better if you stick to mutual funds and put your investments on autopilot?

Next, we'll look at your family arrangements. How do you protect your own welfare and that of your loved ones when you marry, divorce, live in a common-law relationship or become widowed? What are the best ways to save for children's post-secondary education? How do you practise safe income splitting to pay less in taxes?

Finally, we're at the final stage of life. Death and disability are uncomfortable subjects, so it's only natural to avert your eyes. But that's how you can get into financial trouble, by failing to plan or not sharing your plans with your family.

We'll take a clear-eyed look at writing a will, developing an estate plan and appointing someone to make decisions on your behalf if you're sick or mentally incapacitated. At the end, you'll be aware of the risks of doing nothing, and you'll be motivated to get going.

Money 101 is a journey. And like most journeys, it has a few rough spots. Not everything is smooth sailing. You lose your way sometimes, you get disoriented and you find your arrangements have fallen apart. But you learn to overcome disappointments and get back on track. That's what seasoned travellers do.

I hope you like this book, which started with an idea I had to do a series explaining the basics of money management in a step-by-step fashion every Sunday in the *Toronto Star*. I've updated and expanded the original columns, while adding stories from readers and some of their feedback. There's an enormous appetite for this kind of writing, I found. Readers kept asking for copies, so I figured it was time to organize them into a single volume.

The journey continues. *Money 201*, the next instalment, now runs every week in the Toronto Star. It's a more in-depth look at some of the topics covered earlier and some new ones too. I want to thank the editors of the business section, Colin MacKenzie and then Kenneth Kidd, for encouraging me to do the series and Rick Haliechuk, the editor who puts it together each week.

I think of my role as that of navigator, helping you get around the twists and turns of the road and warning you about potholes. Our goal: To drive more safely and stay on the financial straight and narrow.

You make a decent salary, but you spend all you earn and then some. You wish you could put something aside for unexpected expenses. But when your car breaks down or your basement floods, you charge the repairs to a credit card. Gradually, the bills mount up, and you're not comfortable with how much you owe. You want to cut back on your spending, but you're not sure where the money goes.

Tracking your expenses is the first step on the ladder to financial well-being. Once you categorize your spending, you can start reducing it. I'm not talking about a slash-and-burn operation, but about a few modest trims here and there. Budgeting that hurts too much is not sustainable.

With better control of your money, you can start a rainy-day fund and save a little for the future. That's your security blanket in case life throws you some curves, a safety cushion that makes you stronger and gives you an alternative to putting everything on plastic.

In this section, I'll also look at how to save money on banking. Many of us drift into a relationship with a financial institution through habit or convenience and end up paying more than we should. It's important to pick the right bank products and services, then stay on top of what you're paying. To get a better deal, you may have to do some of the work yourself or venture outside of the big banks.

Debit cards can also be dangerous to your financial health if used carelessly. We'll give you tips to prevent thieves from getting access to your debit card and personal identification number.

Insurance is another key part of your financial foundation. It helps protect you against adversity and maintains your lifestyle in case of death, accident, illness or theft. But you have to pick the right insurance policy and the best level of coverage. Otherwise, you may be wasting your money.

Finally, we'll look at how your savings are protected if a financial institution goes out of business. The compensation depends on where you keep your money and how much is in your account, so you need to tailor your savings accordingly.

Keep track of
your spending

Do you know your true cost of living? Unless you keep every receipt and write down details every time you open your wallet, you probably don't have an accurate picture.

You may remember the big-ticket items—rent or mortgage payments, groceries, utility bills—but lose track of how much you dribble away on extras.

Want a surprise? Record every penny you spend and see where the money goes. Do it for at least a month. Three months is better, but you'll probably get bored.

"People tell us it's a lot of work to record everything they spend," says Laurie Campbell, program manager at the Credit Counselling Service of Toronto, which helps overextended borrowers. "I've done it myself and I can tell you it's no fun."

Budgeting programs such as Quicken or Microsoft Money are great, but they cost at least $60 or $70. And you still have to transfer the information to a computer. Nothing can replace a pen and notebook to record expenses as you go.

Carry your notebook with you and jot down everything you spend (with sales taxes). Write down whether you use cash or cheques, credit cards or debit cards. And make sure to include transactions where you arrange for payments to be taken directly from your bank account.

If you track spending for only a month, no doubt you'll miss a few things. So keep a separate list of expenses that crop up unexpectedly or occur only once or twice a year. I'm talking about professional fees, home and car repairs, furniture, vacations, gifts and donations.

Be honest. "You're always on your best behaviour when there's monitoring going on," Campbell says. "Don't cut back. Spend as usual." Be vigilant about not letting things slip through the cracks.

- When you eat in a restaurant or get your hair cut, don't forget the tip.

- Jot down the loose change you give to your kids or people on the street.

- Include the fees for automatic teller machines not owned by your bank.

Then add up the totals and be prepared to gawk at the results. You'll probably find you lose a lot through "leakage," relatively small amounts spent on purchases such as snacks at work, CDs, videos and paperback books. These expenses mount up.

Find areas where you can cut back

Once you track your expenses for a month or two, you'll see where the money is going. This will help you decide if you're overspending in certain areas and if there's room to squeeze something out.

The goal is to gain better control of your money, so you'll have more to save and invest. Don't call it budgeting, which implies restraint and self-denial. Call it cash-flow management that keeps money from slipping through your fingers.

I'm not advocating that you wipe out all the things that make you happiest. If you find a caffe latte or cappuccino makes you work more efficiently, then keep that three-dollar daily expense in your budget. Everyone needs a little luxury.

But if the bill for fancy coffees seems high relative to your take-home pay, try to cut out one a week and bring your own beverage to work. If you spend too much on the latest books (that's my vice), buy fewer each month and check out bestsellers from the library.

You don't want to feel you're skimping on small pleasures. That's a recipe for failure. You're just trying to rein in costs a little. Taking baby steps, or cost-cutting by increments, works better than slashing entire categories of spending.

Let's focus on an area where it's shamefully easy to go overboard: eating out, takeout and last-minute food purchases. Here are ways to finagle your food budget:

- Eat breakfast at home. If there's no time, pack it up and take it to work. And buy a covered coffee cup or thermos. Fill up at home and drink en route to work.

- Restaurant servings are often big enough for two. Dig into an appetizer for dinner, or share appetizers and main courses with a companion.

- Start bringing your lunch to work. The $5 to $8 you spend on takeout is costing $100 to $120 a month, enough for one really great meal at a fantastic restaurant.

- If you must have chips in the afternoon, buy a big bag at the supermarket and take a little bit to work. It's cheaper than buying from a vending machine.

- Shop with a buddy. If 12 rolls of toilet paper are too much, split with a friend. Single people who buy individual-size servings get hit hard at the grocery store.

- Eat vegetarian more often. Meatless meals are less expensive and healthier than burgers and fries. If you're a sworn meat eater, veg out three times a week.

- Save containers for leftovers and to store dried goods like rice, which are cheaper to buy in bulk than prepackaged.

Finally, learn how to cook. On weekends, prepare a large quantity of one dish. Chili, maybe. Next weekend, lasagna. Then, meatloaf. Package everything in meal-size portions and put them in the freezer. Eat from your stockpile a few nights a week. That alone will save you hundreds of dollars a year.

You're frugal with food? Then try to trim costs on something else where you tend to splurge (such as music, movies, haircuts or clothes). Shifting your spending shouldn't hurt much, if you set firm limits and remember why you want to save.

Here are a few steps that can help put more money in your pocket immediately:

1. Pay off your credit card balances. Trim a little from your monthly miscellaneous expenses and begin paying more than your monthly minimum on each card as quickly as possible. Remember, paying off your credit card balance can be one of the highest-yielding investments you can make.

2. If you can't pay off your balance, transfer your credit card debt to a card that charges a lower interest rate. When checking for a new card, make sure that you'll get the lower rate you want for at least six months. If you have a good history of timely payments with your own credit card company, call and ask them to lower your interest rate and lower or waive some of the fees in return for your continued use of their card. Many companies are willing to do so.

3. Pay bills on time and avoid costly late payment fees.

4. Check your utility bills. Taking even a few simple steps can add up to hundreds of dollars in savings. For example, lower your hot

water heater to 120 degrees Fahrenheit (which is recommended for families with small children anyway) and you can save 10 to 15 per cent. Turn off lights when you are not in the room. Check with your electric or gas company to see if you can save money by doing your laundry or dishwashing at non-peak times.

5. Review your phone bill to see how much you're paying for services that you don't really need. Your phone company can help you choose a calling plan that may give you better rates for the calls you typically make. Check out what you're paying for long-distance fees. Often phone companies will reduce your rates if you call to say you're considering switching to a cheaper plan offered by a competitor.

6. Make one extra mortgage payment per year. Write "to principal" in the memo portion of the cheque so your bank will know you want to apply the entire amount to your principal. By lowering your principal, you're also lowering the amount of interest you owe on your mortgage, which can lead to substantial savings and can cut years off your mortgage.

7. Review your insurance policies. Are you paying for more coverage than you need? By visiting Web sites like www.kanetix.com, you can comparison shop for many types of insurance policies (including term life insurance, homeowners insurance, automobile insurance and travel insurance). It's worth a few minutes of research to determine if you could lower your monthly insurance rates and still receive the coverage you and your family need.

Get the best deal on banking

Are you paying too much for basic banking services? Those nickel-and-dime service charges taken from your account each month add up to a chunk of change over a full year.

Service charges are lucrative for Canada's banks. The bulk of their earnings now come from fees, rather than the spread between what they pay on deposits and what they charge on loans.

If you hate being dinged for each transaction, there are ways to cut the cost of service charges. You can hold a minimum balance of $1,000 or sign up for a low-cost package plan.

Depending on the bank, about half of all customers don't pay any fees, says the Canadian Bankers Association. To help you squeeze into that group, the CBA publishes a guide called "Getting Value for Your Service Fees." Call 1-800-263-0231 or find it at the Web site, www.cba.ca.

There's a consumer profile you can fill out to analyze your banking habits and pick the best service package for your needs.

Here are a few questions to ask:

- What is my estimated minimum monthly balance?

- How many transactions do I do every month?

- How many times a month do I withdraw money, write cheques, pay bills, transfer money between accounts, or make pre-authorized payments and Interac direct payments?

- How many transactions do I do in the branch and how many do I do on my own, using automated banking machines (ABMs), Interac direct payment, or telephone and Internet banking?

- What extra features do I want in my banking plan (safety deposit box, overdraft protection, cancelled cheques returned, money orders, stop payments, foreign currency, withdrawals at other financial institutions' ABMs, credit card, rewards)?

- Do I want my fees waived if I keep a high minimum balance?

If you're under 19 or over 60, are a full-time student or have little activity (fewer than 10 transactions a month), ask your bank if it offers a free or specially priced plan.

Just because you have a monthly package doesn't mean it's the right one. Your needs may have changed or there may be a newer package that fits you better. You can pay next to nothing or up to $30 a month, depending on your activity and the amount of face-to-face help you want to receive.

In general, people who use electronic banking pay less. Doing all your bank business on the telephone or the Internet means you are less costly to service than those who frequently visit a branch.

If you're paying too much for service, shop around. You may think all banks are the same, but there's enough competition among them to provide a rich variety of offerings.

With a flat-fee package at one of the Big Five banks, you'll pay as little as 17 to 20 cents for non-teller transactions, such as cash withdrawals from an automated bank machine, debit card purchases, account transfers and bill payments. You'll pay twice as much—about 50 cents—if you don't have a package, or if you exceed the number of transactions offered in your package.

The Big Five banks like to boast that customers can bank for free if they maintain a minimum balance in their accounts. But the balance required to waive fees is rising: It's $1,000 for CIBC, $2,000 for Bank of Nova Scotia, $1,000 to $5,000 for TD Canada Trust (depending on the plan) and $1,000 to $10,000 for Bank of Montreal.

Royal Bank is the only one of the Big Five banks with no minimum balance required to waive fees. That bank says only a small percentage of clients keep a high enough balance to qualify, and even those who do find it burdensome to monitor their balance carefully.

With a minimum balance requirement, you have to keep your account above the limit for the entire month. If you slip below for even one day, your monthly banking fees won't be waived. This forces you to keep thousands of dollars in your account, money that may be better used or invested elsewhere.

Industry Canada's Strategis Web site has an interactive calculator that lets you compare monthly financial service charges. It's at www.strategis.gc.ca, and there's a link from the Canadian Bankers Association guide. Once you reveal how you do your banking, you're shown the cost of different plans and what's best for you.

Industry Canada also publishes an annual survey of service fees at 15 financial institutions, using five typical customer profiles: Minimal Transaction Consumer, Average Transaction Consumer, Connected Consumer, Convenience Consumer and Prosperous Branch Consumer. The survey (posted at the Strategis Web site) breaks out costs for those with a monthly balance over $1,000 and those under $1,000.

The 2001 survey showed service charges were stable for customers with minimal transactions and had dropped for connected or self-serve clients (who tend to be younger). Convenience customers generally paid the highest fees, no matter how big their balance.

Even if you don't want to switch institutions, you can still save money by picking a more appropriate package. At the Royal Bank, for example, the monthly service charges ranged from $4 a month for minimal transaction consumers to $19.50 a month for convenience consumers.

Once you have a good banking plan, here are some other ways to save money:

- Try to minimize your trips to the bank machine. Take out more money rather than less, if you can stand the temptation of having it burn a hole in your wallet.

- Use your own bank's machines. When you opt for convenience and use ABMs belonging to other banks, you will pay $1.25 to $1.50 each time.

- Unless you're desperate, avoid independent "white label" ABMs. They have an extra layer of surcharges, money that goes to private owners and retailers that install the machines.

- Consider getting overdraft protection, so that all cheques and pre-authorized payments will be honoured up to a certain limit. This saves you from jumbo service charges when a cheque bounces.

- Instead of writing cheques or withdrawing cash, use Interac direct payment. It's generally cheaper. Some stores allow you to withdraw extra cash along with the debit transaction.

Save money with online banking

The more transactions you do electronically, the less you pay for banking. But that's not the only reason to go the self-service route. It can be more convenient, with no "bankers' hours" on the Internet. And you can get more information about your accounts online than if you visit a branch or use the telephone.

Most major banks have been cutting the cost of online banking. They're passing along their lower overhead and also encouraging customers to do transactions electronically. If you've never done it, it's worth a try.

Here are some tips on getting started:

- It's only natural to be concerned about safety. Closely review your bank's privacy and security policies "to see where its liability ends and yours begins," says *MoneySense* magazine. "Online banking security is a shared obligation between you and your bank."

- You'll need a computer with a 32-bit browser with 128-bit strong encryption. Both Netscape Navigator and Internet Explorer supply 32-bit browsers that support 128-bit encryption, so it's your responsibility to download and install one of them. This ensures that your connection to the Internet is as secure as possible.

■ Follow the bank's instructions for protecting your data. Log out after you end your session or if you're interrupted in midstream. Otherwise, family members or co-workers who share your computer may be able to get access to your account information by clicking your browser's Back button.

■ If you can't find answers to your questions at a bank's Web site, check www.moneysense.ca; see the section on Banking and Credit. There's a guide to Web banking, with contact information for 10 of the major banks.

TD Canada Trust scored highest in a survey of online banking by *MoneySense* in August 2001. Bank of Montreal came a close second. Royal Bank was cited for email support, since it sent a full response to a query (not an automated response) in just four hours.

The Big Five banks are feeling pressure from virtual banks, such as President's Choice Financial, Citizen's Bank of Canada and ING Direct. If you rarely or never visit a branch, there are major bargains to be had by switching to a virtual bank. You'll find the service charges can be a good deal lower.

Customers of President's Choice Financial pay no fees, no matter what their balance. They also collect "PC points," which they can redeem for groceries at Loblaws stores. Meanwhile, Citizens Bank has no fees for customers with more than a $1,000 monthly balance.

Virtual banks pay higher rates on savings, too, usually on the first dollar you deposit. There's no minimum balance or tiered rate system, as at the Big Five banks. Without a branch network across the country, they can pass the cost reductions along to customers.

ING Direct, a subsidiary of a huge Dutch company, is the leader in offering higher savings rates. Since June 2002, it has been paying 2.75 per cent on savings. Not only is this more than what major banks pay on short-term savings, it's better than the 2 per cent they pay on a guaranteed investment certificate that is locked in for one year.

Other virtual banks that pay higher rates on savings include Achieva Financial, Amex Bank of Canada, Finactive, MRS Trust and Manulife Bank.

It's a no-brainer to park your short-term money where you earn a decent rate. Don't leave big balances in a chequing or savings account that pays a paltry fraction. So get moving. You can open an account at a virtual bank without giving up your other banking arrangements.

Many newspapers publish a table of interest rates once a week. On the Internet, the most detailed numbers are at www.cannex.com, where financial institutions enter and update their own interest rates. You can also find rate comparisons at www.webfin.com, www.moneysense.ca and www.money.msn.ca.

In return for higher savings rates at virtual banks, you do sacrifice some convenience. When making a deposit, you can't just walk into a branch and hand over a cheque. You must transfer money from an account at another financial institution, which can take a few days. (But you can have paycheques, pension or investment income deposited directly to your virtual bank account.)

Withdrawing money, too, may take a few days. You can write or endorse a cheque and mail it in, transfer money to an account at another institution or set up pre-authorized payments for bills.

Credit unions are good places to go if you want low-cost banking services. These not-for-profit, community-based institutions strive to be more welcoming and user-friendly than the big banks.

Credit unions are innovative and have led the banks in product development. They introduced daily-interest savings accounts and biweekly mortgage payments, to name a couple of firsts. They were among the first to install ABMs and to provide direct payroll deposit services in Ontario, debit cards in Saskatchewan, telephone banking in British Columbia and online banking in Quebec.

Canada has 2,200 individual credit unions and caisses populaires (found predominantly in Quebec), says the federal finance department. Here are some statistics:

- With 10 million members or about 33 per cent of the population, Canada has the world's highest per capita membership in the credit union movement.

- One-quarter of Canadians use a credit union or caisse populaire as their primary financial institution.

- Credit unions hold about 12 per cent of the domestic assets of Canada's deposit-taking financial institutions.

- The movement is most active in Quebec and Saskatchewan (where it has a 40 per cent market share) and British Columbia (where its market share is 20 per cent).

Credit unions and caisses populaires grew by focusing on areas where commercial banks wouldn't go. They're strong in consumer credit and deposit services, residential mortgages and small business loans. More recently, credit unions have made a name for themselves in branchless banking and ethical mutual funds.

Credit unions are co-operative financial institutions. This means they have members, not customers, who own and control them. Each member has one vote, no matter how big his or her deposits are. Any profits are put back into the community as loans or dividends paid on members' shares.

Consumers rank credit unions far above banks in service. A 2002 study by Acumen Research Group of 2,000 Canadians found they award higher grades to credit unions than to big banks in several areas—making customers feel valued, problem-solving, competitive service fees and interest rates.

You're interested in joining a credit union, but don't know where to find one near you? Don't worry. The Credit Union Central of Canada can help. At its Web site (www.cucentral.ca), you can enter a home or office location and get a map of the credit unions located in the area. I found five within a few kilometres of my home. There's also an ABM locator.

You can also sign up with Citizens Bank of Canada, which was set up in 1997 by the Vancouver City Savings Credit Union. Citizens Bank operates nationally as a virtual institution, with services available only by telephone or Internet. There are no branches.

Citizens Bank offers an $8-a-month banking package for customers with balances of less than $1,000. That's lower than what you'd pay at any of the big banks. Since it has no ABMs of its own,

Citizens allows unlimited access to automated bank machines operated by other banks. If your balance is above $1,000 or you have more than $25,000 in deposits or RRSPs, there are no fees at all.

Another thing that makes Citizens different is the ethical policy that guides all the bank's decisions. It covers eight areas: the environment, human rights, employee relations, sustainable energy, animal testing, military weapons, tobacco and business conduct. For more information, check the Web site (www.citizensbank.ca).

My only quibble is with the low rates paid on savings, which penalize small savers. Citizens Bank has a tiered rate structure, paying interest of 0.5 per cent on balances up to $5,000 and 1 per cent on $5,001 to $25,000. The rate hits 1.5 per cent at $25,000-plus and never goes higher, no matter how high your balance.

As an alternative, Citizens has a one-year term deposit that pays 2.25 per cent on $500 or more. The term deposit is cashable any time after 29 days, so you can get out your money in a financial crunch or reinvest if rates increase.

Take care when using debit cards

Debit cards are a terrific invention. You swipe a card through a point-of-sale terminal and key in a personal identification number, or PIN. Within seconds, money is automatically transferred from your account to the store's account.

Introduced in 1994, debit cards have already surpassed cash as our preferred method of payment. Today, the number of card-based transactions (including debit and credit cards) in Canada is twice the size of paper-based transactions (cash and cheques).

Who wants to carry cash? A wallet full of bills makes you a target for thieves. But debit cards are safer—or so you think. Well, think again. There's something about debit cards you may not appreciate. If someone steals your debit card to take money from your account, you could be held responsible if your financial institution decides the theft was your fault.

Many people don't realize they have unlimited liability. They think debit cards are treated the same way as credit cards. When your credit card is stolen, you're not liable for losses if you report the theft right away. And even if you don't report the theft promptly, you're on the hook for $50 at most.

You can lose much more with a stolen debit card. In fact, your losses can be more than the actual amount of funds in your account. This can happen if you have a line of credit or overdraft protection on the account or if it's linked with other accounts.

You're more likely to be held liable for debit card losses if you haven't taken care of your PIN. It's your electronic signature. Here are some ways to safeguard your confidential number:

- When using a debit card at a store or an automated bank machine, shield your PIN as you enter it. Beware of "shoulder surfers," people who lurk behind you to get a look at your number as you enter it.

- Don't write your PIN on your card or keep a poorly disguised written record in your wallet, purse or briefcase. This is an invitation to thieves to steal your money.

- Don't use a PIN that's easy to identify, such as your birthday, address, telephone number or social insurance number. Scramble the numbers in some way.

- Don't walk away from an ABM or retail checkout without taking your debit card and transaction record.

- Don't give your PIN to anyone who asks you for it, even to the police or your own financial institution.

There's one exception to the non-disclosure rule. If someone holds a gun to your head or a knife to your throat and demands your personal identification number, don't be a hero. Give it to them. You're covered for crime-related losses if you divulge your PIN.

Financial institutions, retailers, governments and consumer groups have endorsed a 10-year-old voluntary code of practice for debit-card services. The code was revised recently to expand on the question of who's liable for losses. A cardholder is not liable for losses if he or she has been "the victim of fraud, theft or has been coerced by trickery, force or intimidation," the code says.

I strongly recommend you read the Canadian Code of Practice for Consumer Debit Card Services. You can find it posted at the Web site of the Interac Association, www.interac.ca, and the Canadian Bankers Association, www.cba.ca. The code defines your responsibilities when you use a debit card to take money from an automated bank machine or to pay for goods or services. If there's a problem, when are you at fault?

For example, suppose you make an error when entering an amount. You deposit $1,000 at an ABM, but you incorrectly enter $100. If one of your cheques bounces before the bank has a chance to verify the funds are there, you're responsible. Because it was your mistake, you have to pay any service charges, interest and fees resulting from not having enough funds in your account.

However, you're not responsible for entry errors and won't have to pay service charges if the message on an ABM "has not been written in clear or understandable language."

So read the code carefully, safeguard your PIN and report problems promptly to the debit card issuer. Your financial health depends on it.

Know how your savings are protected

What happens to your money if a financial institution goes bankrupt? Will you recover all your losses, or will you be out of pocket? Which deposits are protected and which are not?

Your financial institution should be telling you this stuff. But employees are busy and have other jobs to do. They're not always trained or qualified to explain the technicalities. That's why I'm going to make a stab at unravelling the rules. This is important information. So don't skip it.

The money you have on deposit with a financial institution is usually protected by an insurance plan if the company collapses. But each plan has exemptions and coverage limits. You have to know how they work, so you can allocate your money properly.

Let's start with the Canada Deposit Insurance Corp., a federal Crown corporation established in 1967. It has 94 member institutions, which include banks, trust companies and loan companies.

The list of member institutions is available on CDIC's Web site at www.cdic.ca. You can also call CDIC directly at 1-800-461-2342 to find out if a financial institution is a CDIC member. Look for a red and white CDIC decal at the branch. Credit unions are not CDIC-insured, and neither are deposits held by insurance companies.

CDIC insures the following types of deposits: savings and chequing accounts, term deposits such as GICs (guaranteed investment certificates), money orders, cheques and certified cheques.

To be eligible for CDIC protection, the deposit must be in Canadian dollars and must be repayable no more than five years after the date of deposit. That excludes a U.S. dollar savings account, for example, or a long-term GIC that matures in seven or 10 years.

Mutual funds are not insured by the CDIC. Neither are stocks, treasury bills, investments in mortgages, bonds and debentures issued by governments and corporations. Don't be confused by the fact that these investments are sold by CDIC members. They're not eligible for protection.

Suppose you're buying a product at a financial institution and you can't find out whether it's CDIC-insured or not. Ask to see the "deposit register." This is a list of all insured deposits that CDIC members must make available at their branches. If they sell products on the Internet, they must have the deposit register at their Web site.

Here's how CDIC deposit insurance works:

- You don't apply. Eligible deposits with CDIC members are automatically insured.

- The most protection you can have with one institution is $60,000. This coverage applies to all the insurable deposits you have with the same CDIC member.

- The $60,000 limit covers interest, as well as principal. So you should invest only $50,000 to $55,000 with one institution and leave a cushion for growth of your money.

- Deposits held in RRSPs (registered retirement savings plans) and RRIFs (registered retirement income plans) are insured separately.

- Deposits held in RESPs (registered education savings plans) are not insured separately.

The CDIC used to keep a low profile. That changed in 2000, when it launched a five-year public education campaign. I find the

TV commercials annoying, but I'm relieved to see CDIC come out of the closet. It had to clear up the confusion after a public opinion survey showed only one in four Canadians knew mutual funds were not insured.

To see how much you know about deposit insurance, go to www.cdic.ca and take the quiz. There are 10 multiple-choice questions. Most people get only five or six right, the CDIC said at the beginning of the campaign.

While you're at the Web site, try out the interactive deposit insurance calculator. It guides you through a set of questions on your deposits and tells you what insurance coverage you would have if the financial institution went under.

Deposits held at credit unions and caisses populaires are not CDIC-insured. Credit unions are members of provincial deposit insurance plans, which provide coverage that is at least as generous as CDIC's and often much better.

Here's how the provincial plans work:

- Alberta, Saskatchewan and Manitoba guarantee 100 per cent of credit union deposits.

- Nova Scotia insures deposits up to $250,000.

- British Columbia and Ontario insure deposits up to $100,000.

- New Brunswick, Newfoundland and Prince Edward Island insure deposits up to $60,000. But PEI insures the total value of RRSP and RRIF deposits.

- Quebec insures deposits up to $60,000.

You can get more information from Credit Union Central of Canada, www.cucentral.ca, which gives details on deposit insurance plans in nine provinces. Also check the Web site of the Financial Consumer Agency of Canada, www.fcac-acfc.gc.ca.

When a life insurance company becomes insolvent, the Canadian Life and Health Insurance Compensation Corp. steps in to protect customers. CompCorp, as it's known, is funded and run by the industry. But every life insurance company in Canada has to join. CompCorp protects each life insurance deposit up to $60,000, including interest. RRSPs and RRIFs are insured separately.

A life insurance company may sell some products that are covered by CompCorp (such as annuities), but it may have a trust company subsidiary that sells other products that are covered by the CDIC (such as guaranteed investment certificates). Ask the company what type of protection you will get.

To see if a life insurance company is a member, call CompCorp at 1-800-268-8099 (416-777-2344 in Toronto) or visit the Web site (www.compcorp.ca).

In a later chapter, I'll look at the Canadian Investor Protection Fund. This is an industry-run plan that protects money in stocks, bonds and mutual fund investments sold by investment dealers.

Put your savings to work

You've started to trim your expenses. What do you do with the money? Let's get some numbers on the table. Suppose you buy a coffee and bagel before work, a sandwich and drink at lunch and a caffe latte after work. That adds up to $10 a day, money that could go into savings or investment or could be used to reduce debt.

By packing your own breakfast and lunch every day, you'll save $25 a week (to be conservative). At the end of the year, you'll have $1,300. That's nothing to sneeze at. But look at what happens when you invest the money.

Contribute $25 a week to a high-growth mutual fund that averages 10 per cent in annual returns. In five years, your money will grow to $8,400. In 10 years, it will grow to $22,300. That's the effect of compounding, when you reinvest your gains year after year.

I admit that 10 per cent a year is on the high side. The best mutual funds will give you a double-digit return, but the average Canadian stock fund hasn't grown as much over the past decade. And, of course, there are five-year periods when many funds struggle to break even.

But you get the picture. Saving and compounding your money will yield more rewards than a daily coffee and bagel. Even if you manage to save just $5 a week, that's not insubstantial. Sock away $250 a year and you'll have something good to show for it in the long term.

So here's the drill: Analyze your monthly expenses and find some incidental spending you can convert into saving. Once you decide on the amount, make your savings goal official. Put a sign on your fridge. Add a picture of what you're saving for: a college education for your kids, a cottage by the lake or chalet near the ski hill, a retirement villa in the south of France.

Then arrange to have the money deducted regularly from your pay or bank account. You want it to go automatically into savings, so it never gets into your hands. For most people, preauthorized chequing works best. Ask your financial institution to debit your account by a chosen amount. Do it weekly, every two weeks or once a month.

The next step is deciding where your savings will go. Mutual fund companies are happy to let you pay a small amount each month. The minimum is usually $100. If you don't know which fund to buy, use a money market fund. That's a short-term parking spot for savings.

Your mutual fund can be set up as a registered retirement savings plan (RRSP). There's no need to wait till January or February to contribute. You can start a plan at any time of year.

Think of an RRSP as a big basket that holds a variety of investments. Once the money is inside an RRSP, it's harder to grab in a moment of weakness. Withdraw money and you pay at least a 10 per cent tax right off the top. And you may owe a lot more at income tax time. Not a pretty thought.

You can also use a savings account, preferably one that pays a reasonable interest rate (two per cent or more). When you have enough, move it into a term deposit or guaranteed investment certificate. Locking up your money for the long term, whether inside or outside an RRSP, keeps it safe during your moments of temptation.

**Set aside money
for emergencies**

One reason to start a pay-yourself-first savings program is to put money aside for emergencies. How much is enough? Some financial planners say you should have the equivalent of six months' take-home pay. Others say three months.

The money should go into a savings account or a Canada Savings Bond, something easy to liquidate at a moment's notice if you lose your job or suddenly need to make a major purchase. The problem: The advice is tough to follow and not many people do it.

"I'm not a fan of emergency funds," says David Chilton, author of *The Wealthy Barber*, a bestselling financial planning guide. "I agree you should have a little bit of money around. But if you do it the way they tell you, it becomes a stereo fund or travel fund." In other words, you'll be tempted to use the money for other things. It's human nature, after all, to confuse wants with needs.

There are other ways to cover off emergencies:

- Overdraft protection from the bank will help pay what you owe if you're caught short without enough money in your account. You won't be dinged high fees for bounced cheques and you'll preserve your good credit rating.

- A personal line of credit is offered to higher-income borrowers by financial institutions and credit card promoters. Some credit lines are unsecured, but you can get a lower rate by securing it to your home equity. For emergency purposes, it's best to arrange the credit line before you need it and pay only for what you use. If you have a $20,000 credit line and you use only $1,000 of it, you pay interest just on the $1,000 that's outstanding.

- Premium credit cards often provide a purchase protection plan. If an item you buy is lost, stolen or damaged within the first three or six months, you can ask the credit card company that financed the purchase for reimbursement.

- Gold cards may cover other unexpected expenses, such as out-of-country medical costs or collision damage while you're renting a car. Read the terms carefully to see whether the coverage is worth the cost of the card.

- A margin account with an investment dealer lets you borrow against the value of your holdings. The margin limit is based on the type of security and its market price. You can use that loan for anything, not just investing.

- Certain types of life insurance policies let you borrow against their cash value. But cash-value loans reduce your insurance coverage and you may face an income tax bill if you borrow more than the amount of premiums paid.

Protect yourself with life and disability insurance

If you have a spouse, children or others who depend on your support, they will be left in the lurch if you suddenly lose your income. That's the role of insurance—to provide emergency cash when you're unable to work and provide for your dependents after you die.

Your chances of being disabled before age 65 are twice as high as your chances of dying. So disability is the first insurance you should buy. Yet most people reverse their priorities, buying life insurance long before they think of disability insurance.

The first step: Find out how much insurance you already have under government or employer plans. Employment Insurance and the Canada Pension Plan offer disability benefits. You may be covered by your employer's compensation plan for a work-related injury, but it's hard to collect for job-related illness.

Your employer or union may have a group disability plan, which is the cheapest coverage you'll find. But it covers only 50 to 60 per cent of your pre-tax income, so you may want to supplement it.

If you're self-employed, or change jobs often, consider buying your own disability policy. Disability insurance is fairly expensive. To keep the cost down, choose a longer waiting period for benefits (say, three months or six months). Buy all you can, since it still won't be enough to totally replace your income.

When you're looking for disability protection, you have to know what the policy means by the term "disability." There are three common definitions of disability:

- "Own occupation" or "regular occupation." This means you're unable to perform the duties of your usual job.

- "Any occupation." This means you're unable to work at any job for which you are qualified by education, training or experience.

- "Total disability." This means you're unable to work at any job at all. This tight definition is seldom found in private insurance plans.

The definition of disability is the key to the quality of your plan. It will determine whether or not you'll receive a disability benefit if you're unable to work.

You should look at the time period during which the definition is in effect. Some policies will use the "own occupation" definition for the first two years, but will continue to pay benefits only if you qualify under the "any occupation" definition after that time.

Make sure your policy will pay benefits whether your disability arises from accidents or illness. You want a policy that will cover disability, whatever the cause. Some policies exclude self-inflicted injuries or claims that arise from alcohol or drug abuse. Avoid any policy that won't pay for mental or nervous disorders.

Once you've covered off disability insurance, you can look at whether you need life insurance. Many employers offer life insurance as a benefit. Find out how much life insurance you have on the job and whether you need to top it up.

When deciding how much life insurance coverage you need, there are several considerations: How much of your annual income goes directly to your family's living expenses? How much debt does your family have that would need to be paid off if you died? How much will it cost for your children to go to university? Do you already have insurance or savings set aside? The amount of coverage you need depends on your financial situation, and your family's plans and dreams.

Many life insurance companies offer help to figure out the amount that is best for you. Computerized tools use your personal financial data and—considering inflation, interest rates and other variables—calculate the insurance required to provide your family with the means to carry on, if you die.

Forget about life insurance if you're young, single and have no dependents. If you're a DINK couple (double income, no kids), you may not need insurance either. Each spouse could be self-supporting if the other dies.

Similarly, if you're retired, with grown-up children, life insurance may be of little value to you. Your spouse could have enough to live on, after your death, from government benefits, pensions and savings.

Life insurance is inexpensive compared with disability insurance. The cheapest kind is term insurance. Think of it as a bet. Suppose you're 35, a non-smoker, in good health. A life insurance company will give you odds of 1,000 to one you won't die this year. You pay the insurance company $1 and, if you die during the year, the insurance company pays $1,000 to your survivors. If you live, you lose the bet and the insurance company keeps your money.

Term gets more expensive as you get older. If you're 65, you may have to put up $250 to the insurance company's $1,000 that you will die during the year. Life policies with cash-value components have higher premiums. But some money goes into a savings account that is yours to borrow against or to keep if you cancel the policy.

Cash-value is more affordable if you need insurance into your 70s or 80s. But if you have an average income and a young family to support, you get far more coverage for your money with a term policy. You can compare term insurance prices at www.term4sale.com. Compulife Software Inc. of Kitchener, Ont., which supplies software to insurance brokers, sponsors the Web site and will supply names of three independent brokers in your area. You don't have to give personal details and no one will call you later to sell you insurance.

The Consumer Federation of America in Washington, D.C., recently released a comparative study of 25 Internet sites offering term life insurance information. The results showed tremendous differences in the quality and reliability of these sites in finding the most economical policies.

"Clearly, shopping around can pay off, but the best deal is very much dependent on where you land on the Web," said J. Robert Hunter, the consumer group's director of insurance and report co-author. Some sites were merely referral services to put a consumer in touch with an agent. The highest-rated site was Term4Sale, which was recommended for its complete list of insurers and ease of use.

Another Web site I'd recommend is Insurance Canada, www.insurance-canada.ca, a useful source of consumer information about all kinds of insurance, including life and disability plans. My only caveat: Some articles are written by life insurance companies and reflect their own biases. But Insurance Canada is run independently of the industry and is endorsed by several Canadian consumer groups.

Top up your health insurance

Canada's health-care system guarantees access to medical services. But not everything is covered. You still have to pay for prescription drugs, dental care, glasses and contact lenses, private and semi-private hospital rooms, wheelchairs, artificial limbs and long-term care. That's why many of us turn to health insurance plans purchased by our employers. Check with your employer or your union to see what you're getting as an employee benefit. Find out about deductibles, maximums and exclusions.

If your spouse is employed, you may be tempted to save by opting out of the group plan that provides less generous benefits. But this could be a false economy. Many employers allow you to co-ordinate the benefits. This means you claim expenses from one plan first and then from the second, following insurance industry standards. For example, if you're claiming expenses for your children, and both you and your spouse have coverage under different plans, you claim first under the plan of the parent with the earlier birthday in the calendar year. You may be able to get coverage of 100 per cent of your eligible expenses, which is very useful if someone in your family needs expensive glasses or orthodontic work.

For those who aren't members of a group plan paid for by the employer, there are also group plans available through professional or alumni associations. You pay less than you would for an individual plan because of reduced administrative costs.

Remember that your health coverage ends when you leave your job or quit being a member of the association. But if you are laid off because of downsizing, the benefits may be extended for a few weeks. Replacement coverage may also be available if you apply within a specific time.

You can also buy individual health plans from an insurance agent, broker or company. You may want to consider buying an individual plan if you are not eligible for a group plan or if your group plan doesn't have a type of coverage that is important to you.

Critical-illness insurance is a new product that protects you against the financial strain of a life-threatening disease, such as cancer, stroke and heart-bypass surgery. Some critical illness plans also cover kidney failure, blindness, organ transplants, quadriplegia, paraplegia and dementia (including Alzheimer's disease). HIV/AIDS is rarely covered.

Within 30 days of your diagnosis, you get a lump-sum payment you can use for anything you wish. It can be for alternative therapies not covered by government, domestic help or even vacations. You don't have to get your expenditures approved or provide receipts.

The concept of critical illness insurance came from Dr. Marius Bernard, brother of the famous South African heart transplant surgeon Dr. Christian Barnard. He realized that patients did not lose their lives—but often lost their life savings—after surviving a serious disease. With their immediate costs taken care of, sick people could focus all their energy on getting better.

Critical illness insurance is new and gets lots of press. But don't get carried away. It's something you look at after you put your disability and life insurance into place. Don't give critical illness too high a priority in your financial planning.

Long-term care insurance is another new type of coverage. It kicks in when an older family member can no longer perform the

normal activities of daily life and needs permanent help at home or
in a care facility. A policy could specify that benefits be paid for one
year, two years, five years, or for the insured person's entire life.

When buying health insurance, you should ask these questions:

- What does the plan cover? What does it provide that isn't covered
  under my provincial health plan?

- What is not covered?

- Are there any limitations or conditions?

- Is there a deductible? If so, how much?

- How much will my premiums go up for the same coverage as I get
  older?

- Do I need a medical examination?

- Will the health insurer provide a refund if I don't make claims?

If you have a pre-existing medical condition, you may find health
insurance hard to get. Many companies will exclude that condition
from coverage or turn you down altogether. "The theory is that you
can't buy fire insurance while your house is burning, so you can't insure
against a medical condition that is already evident," say Sally Praskey
and Helena Moncrieff in *The Insurance Book: What Canadians Really
Need to Know Before Buying Insurance* (Pearson Education Canada).

But you can fight an insurance company that accepts you as a customer and later turns down your claim on the basis that you had a pre-
existing condition. Several of my readers successfully argued that their
illness had not been diagnosed when they applied for coverage. If they
had a pre-existing condition, neither they nor their doctors were aware
of it. So they weren't trying to fool the insurance company.

Insure your home and belongings

Whether you're a student heading off to university, a young person renting your first apartment, a newlywed buying your first home, or an empty nester downsizing to a condominium, you need home insurance.

Home insurance is a "package" policy that generally covers not only your house itself (and any detached structures like garages and sheds), but also its contents, whether they're in the house or temporarily away from it. That means if your state-of-the-art skis are stolen while you're in the chalet sipping hot chocolate, they're covered up to the dollar limit specified in your policy.

Or perhaps a thief nabs your luggage during your Florida vacation. Again, your property insurance kicks in. If someone breaks into your car and steals your expensive camera, it would be your home insurance—not your automobile insurance—that would cover the loss.

Home insurance also gives you legal protection in case of accidents. The liability coverage would come to your rescue if someone got injured on your property and sued you, or if you accidentally injured someone or caused damage to a person's property.

Let's say your neighbour trips on the loose board on your step, breaks her leg and decides to sue you for damages. Or you go out of control down a ski slope, accidentally slamming into a bystander and injuring him. In both cases, your insurance would cover the damages you're ordered to pay and the legal fees to defend you in court.

Many young people moving into their first apartment think they don't need home insurance. After all, they may not have much furniture, and they assume the landlord's insurance will cover any major damage to their unit.

But that's not true. If you cause the damage, you're legally responsible for it. Say, for example, you drop a cigarette on the carpet and it starts a fire in the building. You—not your landlord—would be liable for all the damage that you caused. "Obviously, that could amount to a hefty chunk of money," say Sally Praskey and Helena Moncrieff in *The Insurance Book: What Canadians Really Need to Know Before Buying Insurance* (Pearson Education Canada). Praskey is also editor of the Insurance Canada Web site.

As for your possessions, you may not think you own much of value. But it all adds up. Perhaps your CD or video collection alone would cost more to replace than you could afford. Your renter's or tenant's insurance would replace your belongings if they were stolen or damaged in a fire, plus pay your additional living expenses if you had to live elsewhere while your unit was being repaired. "It's a no-brainer," say Praskey and Moncrieff.

How can you save money on home insurance? Unlike auto insurance, which is regulated by provincial governments, home insurance rates are not regulated. Prices can vary widely. Here are some shopping tips:

- Try getting quotes from different sources: independent brokers (who represent several insurance companies), direct writers (insurance companies that sell through their own agents) and direct-response insurers (who sell over the telephone).

- Ask your auto insurer if it can bundle the policy with home insurance and give you a discounted rate.

■ Install safety devices such as burglar alarms, deadbolt locks, smoke detectors and fire extinguishers. Most insurance companies offer a discount for these features.

■ The higher the deductible, the lower the premium. (The deductible is an amount you agree to pay to cover part of the insured loss.) Go up to $500 or even $1,000, since it's not in your interest to make small property claims.

■ You don't have to pay a deductible for liability claims. But when it comes to liability, don't skimp. Coverage of $1 million should be the minimum. In some provinces, you have to buy at least that much.

■ Watch out for low limits on coverage of some valuable items. You may be allowed to claim only a small amount for bicycles, jewelry, watches, furs and collections of coins, stamps or cards.

■ If you own valuables, it's worth paying for a "rider" or "floater" on your policy. This is an optional extra that beefs up the coverage. You will be protected for accidental loss, as well as theft, and there's generally no deductible.

■ Keep a written inventory of your belongings. Take photographs or videos of everything in your home and keep them in a safe place. This documentation of what you own will be enormously useful if you ever make a claim on the policy.

The Insurance Bureau of Canada, which represents home insurance companies, has two helpful booklets, "Home Insurance Explained" and "Questions to Ask Your Insurance Representative about Home Insurance." You can call the bureau at 416-362-9528 or 1-800-387-2880, or download the information from its Web site, www.ibc.ca.

Questions to ask about home insurance, supplied by the Insurance Bureau of Canada:

■ Who is covered under this policy?

- What property is covered?

- What "perils" are covered? (A peril is an event, such as fire, theft or wind that can cause damage.)

- What is not covered? (This is called an "exclusion.") Exclusions may apply to the persons who are covered, the property covered, the perils insured against, or the location where the coverage applies. Not every circumstance can be covered by an insurance policy. Normal wear-and-tear and deterioration of property are not insurable; you should check your policy for other exclusions.

- What extensions of coverage are available? (Some policy extensions are automatic, while others are optional and/or conditional. Optional coverage you can buy includes protection for your home office or compensation for damage if there's a flood in your basement caused by a sewer backup.)

- What are the conditions of coverage and what do you have to do to make sure that coverage continues?

- What do you do if there's a loss? How do you make a claim to recover a loss?

Protect your car against theft and accidents

If you drive a car, you must have car insurance. It's a legal requirement. This is unlike home insurance, which is desirable but not mandatory.

Because it's compulsory, automobile insurance is highly regulated by the government in each province and territory. Still, there are many choices you can make when it comes to limits, deductibles and optional coverage.

The first decision to make: Do you want to buy auto insurance through an agent or broker? Or do you want to buy from a company that sells directly to the public? In general, you can save money by not using an agent or broker and buying direct. But this means you're on your own if you have to make a claim or change your policy.

Agents represent a single company and brokers represent more than one company. To find an agent or broker in your community, you can look in the yellow pages of your telephone book. Ask your friends if they know of someone they would recommend. Or, if you know a company you'd like to deal with, call and ask for the name of a representative in your area.

A good way to save money on car insurance: Raise the deductible. (The deductible is the portion of the insured loss you pay yourself.)

The higher the deductible, the lower the premium, as a general rule.

A common collision deductible is $300. This means you pay $300 of any repair bill and your insurance company pays the balance. If there's damage that costs less than $300, it's your own responsibility. You can save money by opting for a $500 or $1,000 deductible. If you have an old car, it may not be worth having collision coverage at all.

But don't skimp on third-party liability insurance. This covers you if your vehicle injures someone else or damages his or her property and you are held legally liable. If a claim against you is more than your level of coverage, you can be held personally responsible for the balance. It's smart to buy more than the minimum coverage required by law—$50,000 in Quebec, $200,000 elsewhere. I'd suggest going up to $1 million.

Here are other tips for lowering costs:

- Find out if you're eligible for any discounts. Some discounts for which you may be eligible include multi-car discounts, group discounts, retiree discounts, renewal discounts or young driver discounts.

- Let your broker, agent or insurance company know whenever you make major changes in your life, such as moving, selling your car, cutting back on the number of drivers in your household or substantially reducing your annual mileage.

- If you pay by cheque or automatic withdrawal from your bank account, make sure you always have enough money to cover the payments. Your car insurance policy may be cancelled for non-payment of premiums. And if you have to buy new insurance, you could end up paying higher rates because you're considered a higher risk.

- Drive safely. Your premiums generally rise if you have at-fault automobile accidents and traffic convictions.

- Think about insurance costs before you buy your car. Talk to an agent or broker about the relative costs of insuring different makes and models.

Prepare to pay more if you own a vehicle that is costlier to repair, has fewer safety features or is more likely to be stolen. Most insurers now calculate premiums using a system that takes into account the model's claims experience, rather than the manufacturer's suggested list price for the vehicle.

This system encourages auto manufacturers to build vehicles that are safer, less damage-prone and more theft-resistant, and rewards consumers for buying them, say Sally Praskey and Helena Moncrieff in *The Insurance Book: What Canadians Really Need to Know Before Buying Insurance* (Pearson Education Canada). But it also means your insurance doesn't necessarily get cheaper as your car gets older.

Vehicles most likely to be stolen: high-performance sports cars and sport utility vehicles. Least likely to be stolen: station wagons and other four-door family models. Flashy is not the way to go if you want to save money on your insurance.

The Vehicle Information Centre of Canada compiles information about the insurance claims experience of most popular new models. Check the Web site (www.vicc.com) under "publications" or write to the VICC at 240 Duncan Mill Rd., Suite 700, Toronto, Ont. M3B 1Z4.

One VICC brochure, "How Cars Measure Up," compares claims costs for collision and theft of cars, vans, sport-utility vehicles and pickup trucks in the most recent model year. Another booklet, "Choosing Your Vehicle," compares insurance premiums for the past five model years. It lists the recent-model cars equipped with anti-theft devices and safety features like airbags and anti-lock brakes.

When shopping around for a car insurance policy, here's a checklist of information you need to have on hand when you ask for competitive price quotes:

- Your car: make, model, year, Vehicle Identification Number (VIN), annual mileage, distance driven one way to work, whether you use your car for business.

- Your current broker, agent or insurance company: name, company, phone number, insurance policy number, coverage, deductibles, your current annual insurance rate.

- You as principal driver: gender, birth date, marital status, driver's licence number, how many years you've been licensed to drive in Canada or the U.S., whether you've received driver training, details of all accidents and claims in the past six years, dates of traffic violations in the past three years.

- Other occasional drivers: same information as above.

The checklist comes from the Financial Services Commission of Ontario's brochure, "Shopping For Car Insurance." You can order it by phone at (416) 590-7298 or read it at the Web site (www.fsco.gov.on.ca).

Be sure to tell your agent, broker or insurance company if you have upgraded electronic equipment or accessories in your car, or if you have made modifications to your engine. You may have to pay a higher premium. But if you don't mention the upgrades, you may not be reimbursed for the full value of your upgraded equipment or accessories if you make a claim.

Finally, don't even try to lie on your application. An insurance company has the right to cancel your coverage if you give incorrect or incomplete information.

To skip the tedium of calling several insurance providers, you can try the national electronic quote service Kanetix, www.kanetix.com, an offshoot of Canada Life Assurance Co. Established in 1999, it brings together more than 30 major insurance providers. Kanetix online quotes are also accessible through Yahoo! Canada, MSN.ca and Canoe's Webfin.com money site. The Consumer's Guide to Insurance, www.insurancehotline.com, provides rates from 35 auto insurance companies. The average motorist using the service saves just over $500, says founder Lee Romanov.

As any experienced driver knows, the cheapest insurer is not always the best for service. You may find the low premiums are more than offset by quarrels about claims or dramatically increased rates afterward.

To learn how well a company handles claims, find someone who had an accident and ask a few questions. Could you call after normal business hours? How quickly was your car repaired? How quickly were your injuries treated? Were you pleased with the service? How did the accident affect your premiums? Another good bet: Ask body shop owners what companies are most co-operative with their clients.

Each year, the Financial Services Commission of Ontario hires an independent research firm to ask customers how satisfied they were with the way their insurance claims had been handled. The 2001 survey, reprinted on the Web site, shows an average 85 per cent customer satisfaction with 47 insurance companies. Many companies that sell directly to the public without using agents (Belair, Certas, RBC General, TD Direct) scored below average.

To learn more about auto insurance, check these Web sites:

- Insurance Canada, www.insurance-canada.ca.

- Insurance Bureau of Canada, www.ibc.ca.

Keep in touch with your auto insurer

If someone living with you cancels a car insurance policy, make sure to tell the old company who's supplying the new coverage. Otherwise, that household member may be added to your insurance policy, without your knowledge or approval.

That's what happened to Taeko, a *Toronto Star* reader. She and and her husband were notified by Certas Direct Insurance in May that their car insurance payments would increase to $250 a month from $150. The reason: Her sister Akiko, who was renting a basement apartment in their house, had been added to the couple's policy.

Akiko had also been insured with Certas, but cancelled because she was unhappy with the rates and service. Unfortunately, she had not given Certas the name of her new insurer.

"If you get car insurance from another company, we want to know," said spokesperson Ginny Snow of Certas, a subsidiary of Desjardins Financial Corp. "Cancelling the policy is not enough."

Insurance companies have to cover their exposure to possible claims. What if Akiko had sold her own car and started driving her sister and brother-in-law's car? Certas would have been liable if Akiko had an accident.

"It's our business practice to add any licensed driver in a household to an existing policy," Snow said.

But Certas didn't cover its bases on the communications front. Days after the couple renewed the policy in early May, a revised statement arrived with the 67 per cent increase—and no explanation. That came by mail only a week later.

Taeko called Certas and got a verbal commitment that her sister would be removed from the policy. The company later reneged and deducted $350 from their bank account for the month of May, $100 more than what had been billed initially.

Calling again and again over two months, Taeko got nowhere. Finally, a supervisor said she would have to provide proof that her sister was insured with another company or had moved out of the house.

"I got angry, since this was extra paperwork generated by Certas for me to pursue," Taeko said. "My sister said that when she cancelled, she was not given any indication that she would be added to her brother-in-law's policy."

Once Taeko threatened to go to the company's ombudsman, the customer relations manager (who had ignored her previous messages) called back right away.

"He was profusely apologetic," she says. "He agreed we should have received a phone call asking our permission to put another person onto our policy."

The lesson arising from this story is to keep track of your household's auto insurance coverage. If a non-family tenant cancels an auto insurance policy and moves out, you may still be on the hook.

And if you want great customer service, think twice about using insurance companies that sell directly to the public without going through insurance brokers and agents. Sure, they generally charge less for the same coverage. But the lower cost may not offset the time you spend trying to resolve problems if anything goes wrong.

Be cautious about buying extended warranties

"Do you want the extended warranty?" The question pops up whenever you buy a stereo, TV, computer or appliance. For $50 to $100 or more, you can supplement the factory warranty with an extra two to five years of coverage for repairs and maintenance.

Retailers have a good reason to push extended warranties: They're extremely profitable. Stores often make more money on these "protection plans" and "service agreements" than on the items covered. Some tie staff pay and promotions to the number of plans sold, and give tips on how to persist in selling a plan even after the consumer has turned it down.

In a 1997 survey, *Consumer Reports* magazine found that readers who bought an extended warranty for an audio-video item paid about as much for the plan, by the time the item broke, as the average repair cost for a product of that age. And in most categories of electronic products, fewer than 25 per cent even required repairs by age five.

Extended warranties, ranging from $500 to $1,500, are also promoted for cars. They're a waste of money if you buy a reliable model and you plan on keeping it only three or four years. Phil Edmonston, author of the popular *Lemon-Aid* new and used car guides, says an extended warranty may be worthwhile for a vehicle with a poor repair history: "But what are you doing buying these cars in the first place?"

Some otherwise reliable minivans, such as the Ford Windstar and Dodge Caravan, have a history of power train problems, says Edmonston. His advice: Buy an extended power train warranty, not the more expensive bumper-to-bumper protection. And try to bargain down the cost, since a third to a half is the dealer's mark-up.

Warranties from independent firms, not tied to a manufacturer or retailer, can be a problem. These companies have a habit of going out of business. Even well-known retailers can go under. When Eaton's closed its doors in fall 1999, the venerable department store chain left about 250,000 appliances and electronics items under extended warranties. These contracts were sold to Mississauga-based Camco Inc., which offered Eaton's customers new extended warranties—at an extra cost.

Consumer Reports singles out two high-priced products—projection TV sets and digital camcorders—for which an extended warranty is worth considering. Each can easily have a price tag in the thousands of dollars and is potentially costly to repair.

When it comes to insurance, skip the little stuff and cover the major risks. Think about self-insuring your purchases. That's what Doug Higgins of Aurora did when he bought a new car two years ago. Instead of paying the dealer $1,200 for an extended warranty, he put $1,200 into a guaranteed investment certificate at the bank and added $100 a month to the GIC through an automatic debit from his account.

"Sure, the interest is paltry but the whole investment, plus interest, keeps rolling over and over. It is disciplined insurance," he says. Higgins wishes he'd done that with his $750 GE fridge, which has now cost $750 in extended warranties through Camco. "Had we started a GIC eight years ago, we'd have a new fridge by now."

part two

Borrowing Money

Buy a house or a car, take a vacation, order concert tickets on the telephone: Chances are you're using credit for all these purchases. Credit is the grease that makes the engine of commerce run smoothly. It's what keeps consumers spending, even when their income drops and they try to cut back. Automakers offered zero-interest loans after the September 11 terrorist tragedy and vehicle sales soared.

Credit can be your best friend or your worst enemy, depending on how you use it. You'll be fine if you don't get overextended, you make your payments promptly, and you take advantage of prepayment privileges. And don't forget to shop around for rates. Lenders will negotiate if they think you're a good customer—they will want your business. Even credit card issuers will sometimes knock a point or two off the rate if you ask.

But you can get in trouble if you're not careful with credit. Never borrow as much money as lenders want to give you. Make sure you know your limits. Notify your creditors right away if you lose your job or can't make your payments for other reasons.

About 68 per cent of households have some outstanding debt, according to Statistics Canada. While most can handle their debts, about 30 per cent of households feel uncomfortable with their debt load. About 14 per cent of households are more than two months behind in their payments. And five per cent of households have members who have declared bankruptcy at some time in their lives.

In this section, we'll look at how to handle credit responsibly so it doesn't ruin your life. Shopping for a mortgage is the first order of business. Then we wheel over to car loans and car leasing. Then we compare credit cards and help you decide whether to go for rewards or rates.

Finally, we'll tell you how to interpret your credit score and how to check with the credit bureau to make sure the information is accurate. A good credit rating is a prime asset, a precious jewel that, once tarnished, is hard to shine up again. Treat credit with care so you're in control. That's the key to financial success.

Shop around for a mortgage

When buying a house, you look at dozens of properties before finding one you like. You go around with a real estate agent for months and months—and sometimes you still don't buy anything. Finally, you locate the right home at the right price. You make an offer and the seller agrees. It's an exhilarating, scary, busy, crazy time.

Your to-do list is several pages long, full of big jobs. You need a mover, painter, electrician, plumber, carpet cleaner and so on. There's no time to think.

The mortgage? No sweat. You're already pre-approved for what you need. You just go to the bank and sign.

Hold on. Not so fast.

Now you have the home of your dreams, don't you want the loan of your dreams? What happened to shopping around?

There's more to a mortgage than a low rate. Flexibility is just as important. You want to find a lender that offers a good balance between both. Your mortgage should offer maximum flexibility, even if it carries a slightly higher interest rate.

This is the biggest financial obligation of your life. You can discharge it slowly or quickly. Take the scenic route or the highway: It's your choice.

Normally, you pay off the mortgage over 25 years. By the time you're done, you have handed over three times as much as you borrowed. A $150,000 home has cost you $450,000.

But if you take the fast track, you use every chance you get to prepay the mortgage and reduce the principal. It's one of the best investments you can make. Here's why.

Suppose your mortgage has a 6.5 per cent rate. If you put down $1,000 a year toward the principal, you save $65 in after-tax cash. Big deal, you say. Who cares about $65 a year? It's peanuts.

OK, here's another way to look at the value of prepayments.

What's your marginal tax rate? Let's say 40 per cent. This means for every extra $1 you earn, you lose 40 cents to taxes.

To pay the $65 interest on that $1,000 of mortgage principal, you'd have to earn $108.33 a year. So, your return for prepaying is 10.83 per cent before tax and 6.5 per cent after tax.

That's a whole lot better than the 4 or 5 per cent before tax (and 2 to 3 per cent after tax) you typically earn on investments like bonds and guaranteed investment certificates.

Here are ways to become debt-free as soon as possible:

■ Increase your payments as your income goes up. If things change and you can no longer afford the higher amount, most lenders will let you return to the previous level.

■ Instead of making a monthly mortgage payment, pay every two weeks. That gives you two extra payments each year that go entirely to pay off the principal. If you make monthly payments on a $100,000 mortgage at six per cent, your balance after 10 years is $76,178.08. With biweekly payments on the same mortgage, your balance is only $67,328.08 after 10 years and you pay off the mortgage three years sooner.

■ Use double-up privileges wherever possible and avoid any skip-a-payment feature unless it's absolutely necessary.

■ If you get a tax refund, use it to prepay your mortgage.

■ Use any other cash windfalls, such as a year-end bonus, to make mortgage prepayments.

A mortgage with a variable rate also helps reduce your debt more quickly. The payment is fixed and never changes. When rates fall, more of the payment goes toward the principal. And when rates rise, more goes toward interest.

As with a floating-rate car loan, a floating-rate mortgage is best suited to times when the Bank of Canada rate is on the way down. Watch carefully to see when it's time to lock into a fixed rate. You can tolerate small ups and downs, but you don't want to float when rates are rising steadily.

You can find up-to-date mortgage rates at www.moneysense.ca, www.webfin.com and www.cannex.com. Remember these are the posted rates, not necessarily what you will pay.

If you're a good customer of a financial institution, you can easily negotiate a quarter-point to a half-point discount. Sometimes you can get as much as a full percentage point off the posted rate if you know how to haggle. Your best bet is to package your business. It may make sense to consolidate your car loan, chequing and savings accounts, credit cards and RRSPs with a single lender in order to get a lower mortgage rate.

"Show the bank that it should not look at your application for the mortgage alone, but instead see you as needing a whole package of financial services," says Toronto real estate lawyer Howard Turk in *Home Free: Everything You Need to Know about Buying and Selling a Home* (Prentice Hall Canada).

Banks love this because they know that once they've got you, chances are you'll never leave. Moving accounts around is too much of a pain. Even if you switch your mortgage to another lender in the future, you'll probably keep your other business with them.

If you're uncomfortable with negotiating, think about using a mortgage broker to help you get a better deal. I'm not talking about the old-fashioned mortgage broker, who works with problem borrowers and finds private investors who want to lend money. Today, most mortgage brokers work with clients who can get loans anywhere. They negotiate on your behalf with financial institutions, using new technology to get up to 40 lenders bidding for your business. Then you can pick the bid you like best.

You can try out some Canadian mortgage brokerage chains online at www.themortgage.com and www.mortgagecentre.com. These Web sites help you do some research before shopping, such as seeing how much house you can afford and how big your payments will be. About 25 per cent of first-time buyers consult a broker when arranging their financing. Since they're inexperienced, they welcome the personal service. But mortgage brokers get little repeat business.

Nine out of ten Canadians renewing their mortgages go back to the same financial institution they had before, according to a survey by the Canada Mortgage and Housing Corp. Amazingly, 60 per cent of renewal customers take the first offer they're given.

This doesn't make sense. When you go to a bank, trust company or credit union, you have only one lender's products to choose from. You're often pressured to buy whatever the bank is pushing, be it short-term loans or variable rates or cash-back offers.

Mortgage brokers deal with many different types of lenders, and offer a choice of products and rates. Most important, they're sitting on the same side of the table you are. They have nothing to sell but their expertise in negotiating with lenders on your behalf. They take time to explain the fundamentals: down payments, prepayment privileges, high-ratio mortgages, second mortgages, vendor take-back mortgages and the RRSP home buyer's plan. And you don't pay for this advice, since mortgage brokers get a commission from lenders when they make a deal.

Sometimes mortgage brokers will charge fees to higher-risk borrowers who have been turned down for bank financing. Make sure to ask questions about how they get paid. Brokers' fees are not regulated, but the cost of borrowing must be disclosed on your mortgage documents. The Canadian Institute of Mortgage Brokers and Lenders (CJMBL) enforces a set of ethical guidelines for its members. For information, call 1-888-442-4625 or check the Web site, www.cimbl.ca. CIMBL also has a number of useful online mortgage calculators.

If online calculators aren't enough, you might want to check out a couple of Canadian software products that are sold online. The

Home Calculator is $35 plus tax at www.b4usign.com. Mortgage2 Pro is $39 at www.amortization.com. They can help you do what-if scenarios, trying out different rates and prepayments, and print out amortization schedules.

An RRSP loan can cut mortgage costs

The federal government lets you borrow interest-free and tax-free money from your RRSP to buy a home. You can use this source of financing if you haven't owned a home in the last five years. I'm thrilled the home buyers' plan is a success, since I lobbied for it in my columns. Home ownership is the key to financial security, just as important as setting up a registered retirement savings plan. One million Canadians have benefited from the plan since 1992.

You can use the RRSP loan for anything, but many people add it to their down payment. In that way, they avoid a costly second mortgage or high-ratio loan insured by the Canada Mortgage and Housing Corp.

Home buyers can put down a five per cent down payment if the loan is CMHC-insured (to protect the lender against default). But the insurance premium is high.

For example, if you put down five per cent and take out a high-ratio mortgage of $150,000, the cost is 3.75 per cent (or $5,625). You pay the money up front or else the lender adds it to your mortgage amount.

With a bigger down payment, the insurance cost drops. If you can put down 20 per cent with the help of the RRSP, your CMHC premium drops to 1.25 per cent. On a high-ratio mortgage of $130,000, the cost is a more affordable $1,625.

Of course, if you can bump up your down payment to 25 per cent, you won't need a high-ratio mortgage at all.

Here's a brief description of the plan. For more details, contact the Canada Customs and Revenue Agency (www.ccra-adrc.gc.ca).

- You and your spouse can each withdraw up to $20,000 from your RRSPs. That's up to $40,000 per couple.

- You have to sign a written agreement to buy or build a home.

- You have to start using the home as your principal residence no later than one year after buying or building it.

- You have to repay the amounts borrowed from your RRSP within 15 years. The repayments start about three years after you withdraw the money.

- If you skip a repayment, the money is considered an RRSP withdrawal. It's taxed as income for that year and can't go back into the plan.

Even if you religiously repay the money borrowed from your RRSP, there's still a cost. It's the interest your RRSP gives up and all the future growth on that money. The cost is even higher if you can't make new RRSP contributions because of the required repayments.

You can control the damage to your RRSP by reinvesting the money you save. Since you're paying less each month on your mortgage, you can put that money back into your RRSP or your mortgage. You can also use the savings to buy non-RRSP investments.

Take your savings and buy mutual funds outside your RRSP, advises Gordon Pape in *Retiring Wealthy in the 21st Century* (Pearson Education Canada). You will end up with a tax-paid sum of money that may be worth more than the amount lost to your RRSP, since capital gains are more lightly taxed.

This works only if you're self-disciplined. Many first-time buyers find it a stretch just to repay their RRSP each year, let alone make new RRSP contributions and invest outside an RRSP.

But the beauty of the federal plan is that it lets average Canadians lower their mortgage costs and build equity for retirement. If you have limited income and can't decide whether to save for a home or put money into an RRSP, you can have it both ways. Your money goes into the RRSP, but you still get to use it for a home.

Are you pre-qualified or pre-approved?

Banks love to get new mortgage customers. A popular gambit is to tell people they're approved for a loan of a certain size within a certain time period. If you're a first-time buyer with a small down payment, don't put too much trust in a pre-approved mortgage. Banks may tell you how much you can spend on a house and pull back later, when all the paperwork and credit checks have been done.

This is what happened to Rose and Matt, an engaged couple in their 20s looking for their first house. They had a pre-approved mortgage from the Toronto-Dominion Bank (now TD Canada Trust). So they agreed to waive a condition in their offer that would let them cancel the deal without penalty if the financing fell through. But a pre-approved mortgage is not a binding commitment. TD reneged when it found out the couple's true income. As a result, Rose and Matt ended up losing their $10,000 house deposit.

The bank made a $2,000 settlement after I intervened, but without admitting it did anything wrong. "These young people could be customers of the bank for years to come, so we're doing this strictly as a gesture of customer service," said TD ombudsman David Fisher. His advice to first-time buyers: Read everything in detail. Talk to your lawyer. And if your financing is not guaranteed, don't go in with a firm deal.

Rose and Matt admit they should have taken more care to read the papers they signed. But they got the message there would be no problem with financing if they bought a house in the $200,000 price range. "We feel we were misled by the direct assurances of the bank manager," they told Fisher.

The story provides lessons about what not to do when buying a home.

Lesson One: Don't misstate your income. Rose earned $29,000 a year as a store manager. Matt, who was self-employed, had a business that grossed almost $50,000 a year. The pre-approved mortgage was based on a combined income of $80,000. But it was conditional on Matt's submitting his tax returns and assessments for the previous three years showing his net income.

The couple went ahead and bought the house before submitting the tax returns which showed Matt's income after business expenses averaged less than $20,000. "The income information is where the whole thing fell apart," Fisher says.

Self-employed people often hire an accountant who structures their affairs to show low income. This is "great for keeping the tax collector at bay, but lousy for trying to convince a bank to loan you money to buy a house," says Toronto real estate lawyer Howard Turk, author of *Home-Free: Everything You Need to Know about Buying and Selling a Home* (Prentice Hall Canada).

A self-employed person can still buy a home and get a mortgage, Turk says, but might have to do it a bit differently. A good mortgage broker can shop the application to a number of secondary lenders, usually small trust companies or insurance companies. If that doesn't work, the broker can look for funding in the private mortgage market.

Lesson Two: Don't count on a high-ratio mortgage. Rose and Matt had only $10,000 in savings and couldn't get a conventional mortgage, which requires a 25 per cent down payment. They hoped to put down 5 per cent of the purchase price under the CMHC's insured-loan program.

TD agreed to give them a $212,687 mortgage, which included a 3.75 per cent insurance premium. But the deal depended on CMHC approval. Once the tax returns were submitted, CMHC turned down the deal because the couple's income was too low. The bank then asked for a 25 per cent down payment ($51,250) and a co-signer. A mortgage broker they consulted asked for a 15 per cent down payment. Rose and Matt wanted to buy a house without help from their families. Without a high-ratio mortgage, there was no deal.

Lesson Three: Don't sacrifice your deposit. Rose and Matt agreed to make a firm offer with no conditions. They waived a home inspection and refund of their deposit if the deal collapsed. They don't remember reading or being told what they were signing.

Their real estate agent said he explained the financing waiver and told them he'd be more comfortable with a firm commitment from the bank. "They told me they didn't feel it would be any problem getting satisfactory financing," he said. The Real Estate Council of Ontario dismissed the couple's complaint.

Rose and Matt later broke up, after being together eight years. Their blunder into the housing market helped precipitate the split, says a family member. They could have spared themselves disappointment by consulting a lawyer before buying a house—and not relying on a bank manager's verbal assurances.

Buyer, beware. You won't always get the loan the bank promises. You may be pre-qualified, as in this case, but not pre-approved.

Pre-qualification is an estimate on a mortgage commitment. It's an indication you'll get a loan for a certain amount, based on credit information to be confirmed by a third party. The income details you supply may not check out.

A pre-approved mortgage is a true commitment, but it can also fall through. There may be several reasons, Turk says:

- The home you want to buy doesn't pass the appraisal. The bank may think the price is too high.

- You may have passed the lender's pre-approval process, but not passed the high-ratio insurer's standards.

- If you've switched jobs after you've been pre-approved, your loan may be declined at the last minute.

Here's a quirk you need to know. If you're pre-qualified for a mortgage, you may not have been asked to sign anything. You're not obligated to take the lender's mortgage and you're free to shop around.

You have to be careful, though: "Be warned that you may be making a big mistake by shopping around too much!" Turn cautions. The problem is that lenders do credit checks when you apply for a mortgage. Too many people looking at your credit could mean something is wrong with it. So credit bureaus will cut your credit rating when too many financial institutions ask for it.

You're OK if all the credit requests come in during a 10-day period and relate to the same transaction. Do your shopping within a limited time frame, Turk advises. Or use a mortgage broker, since a broker can submit your application electronically to up to 40 lenders with only one hit to your credit score.

Finally, if you're pre-qualified or pre-approved and your loan is turned down at the last minute, be prepared to find a co-signer. This is someone who will guarantee your payments if you default. You may have friends or family members willing to help.

Save money on your car loans

A car is the second-largest purchase you will make, next to buying a home. Cars are expensive, yet most Canadians find vehicles essential—and almost everyone pays for them with borrowed money.

To minimize the cost of ownership, it's essential to shop for the lowest-priced loan you can get. No matter whether you get financing from a bank or a car dealer, the rate you pay depends on what lenders think of you.

You're graded on "the five Cs of credit," says Gail Vaz-Oxlade in her book, *Shopping for Money: Strategies for Successful Borrowing* (Stoddart).

Character. Lenders look at how often you change jobs, how long you live in the same place and how promptly you repay other debts.

Capacity. Lenders look at how much you earn, how much existing debt you have and how much a new debt will strain your cash flow.

Credit history. Lenders look at your previous loans with them and analyze information provided by a credit-reporting agency.

Capital. Lenders look at your net worth, the value of your assets less your liabilities. "It's what you own minus what you owe," says

Vaz-Oxlade, personal finance columnist for *Chatelaine* magazine.

Collateral. Lenders look at your willingness to pledge your assets as security. These assets, or collateral, can be sold to repay the loan if you default.

If you have a low score on the five Cs, you may be charged a higher interest rate or turned down for credit altogether.

Check your credit rating (more on this later) to make sure all the information about you is correct. To qualify for the best rate on a car loan, you want to clean up your credit history a few months ahead of time.

Here's a good car-buying rule: Make a down payment of 20 per cent or more and finance your vehicle for no longer than four years. You can easily get into trouble when you put little money down and sign on for an auto loan of five years or more. Before you know it, you're "upside down," owing more on a car than it's worth.

Because cars depreciate rapidly in the early years of ownership, it's not unusual for someone to be "upside down" a couple of years into a five-year or six-year loan.

"This is not a good place to be, especially if you decide to trade in the car for another one and have to roll the old car's remaining debt into a new loan," says Bankrate.com, a leading independent Web resource on consumer credit.

"To avoid such a fate, never finance a car for more time than you think you want to own it and opt for the biggest down payment and shortest term possible. Pay ahead whenever possible."

When deciding on a loan term, it's helpful to see what happens to your payments when you stretch them out over a longer period. Suppose you borrow $20,000 at an interest rate of nine per cent. If you opt for five years instead of four years, how much lower will your monthly payments go? And what's the impact of a longer payment period on your total borrowing cost? You can find the answers to these questions by using an Internet loan calculator. I used the one at TD Canada Trust's Web site (www.tdcanadatrust.com).

By taking a year longer to repay the loan, your payments drop by $82.55 a month. The cost is $497.82 a month for a four-year term and $415.27 a month for a five-year term. That $82.55 a month isn't a big difference, about $2.75 a day. Can you squeeze your other costs to accommodate it?

With a shorter-term loan, you save more than $1,000 in total borrowing costs ($3,895.36 over four years vs. $4,916.20 over five years). The result: Interest on your new car represents 20 per cent of the total purchase cost, instead of 25 per cent. That's a big deal. (I've assumed in this example that you pay the same interest rate for a four-year loan as a five-year loan. Some lenders charge a higher rate if you extend the term.)

Here's another way to cut your interest cost over the long run: Opt for more-frequent loan payments. Instead of paying once a month, ask the lender if you can pay weekly, every two weeks or twice a month.

Financial institutions calculate the interest on the declining balance. Since your principal goes down each month, the interest you pay also goes down. If you make 26 biweekly payments, instead of 12 monthly payments, more of your money goes to paying off the principal. As a result, your interest costs shrink.

Instalment loans come in two types, fixed rate and variable rate. You're better off with a fixed-rate loan when interest rates are rising. Variable-rate loans are best when interest rates are stable or falling.

Suppose you take out a variable-rate loan at 10 per cent on January 1. If the rate drops a quarter percentage point on January 15, your loan will be adjusted down to 9.75 per cent in February. But your payment amount won't change. Instead, more of your payment will be applied to the principal, since less is needed to cover the interest cost.

What happens if the rate rises to 10.25 per cent on January 15? Your monthly loan payment may not cover all the interest and you will still owe more at the end of the term.

So watch where interest rates are going. By following the business news, you can spot a trend. If you decide on a variable-rate loan, be sure to lock in when rates appear to be rising.

Another way to reduce interest costs: Opt for a line of credit rather than an instalment loan. With a line of credit, you're approved in advance for a specific amount, say $10,000 or $20,000. You take out as much money as you need and pay only for what you use. The rate fluctuates along with the Bank of Canada rate.

Things to watch for if you use a line of credit:

- Is it secured by collateral or unsecured?

- How much is the minimum monthly payment? (It usually ranges from one to three per cent of the loan amount.)

- Is the payment interest-only or does it include principal? (If you're required to pay only interest, you may never get rid of the loan.)

Not everyone qualifies for a line of credit. Financial institutions require a household income of at least $35,000 to $50,000 a year. And some people get in over their heads with a form of credit that's so accessible and flexible.

Yet another way to reduce costs is the buy-back loan. It's structured like a lease and provides lower monthly payments than a conventional loan. The Royal Bank launched the buy-back loan in 1985. It's also offered by Chrysler Financial Canada (called the Premier Advantage Purchase Plan).

Here's how it works. The bank or financing company establishes the future resale value for your car at the end of the term you choose. Then it deducts that from the amount to be repaid.

Say you're borrowing $20,000 at nine per cent over five years. If the buy-back value of your car is $8,800, you pay interest on $11,200. That lowers your monthly payment to $299, compared to $415 for an ordinary car loan.

However, you still owe $8,800 at the end of the five-year term. This is known as a balloon payment. You have three choices: Pay off the whole amount, try to sell the car for more than the buy-back value or bundle the balance into a new car loan.

Like leases, buy-back loans suit people who want to drive more expensive cars than they can really afford. The "owners" never really own the vehicle. Instead, they refinance every few years.

If you want to get off the revolving debt bandwagon, consider downsizing and driving a less expensive car. That way, you can pay off the loan and still have something to sell at the end of your time of ownership.

Check out zero per cent financing

When the economy slows down, auto makers pull out the big guns. They try to move inventory by offering low-interest or no-interest financing.

But zero-interest deals aren't always the bonus they appear to be. Here are some things to consider:

- Not all buyers qualify for financing. Your credit rating has to be good.

- You may have to make a larger down payment than you would otherwise.

- You may end up paying the sticker price for the car, rather than having the option of negotiating for a better deal.

- Many programs don't offer financing beyond three years. The monthly payments may be more than you can afford to pay.

- The low-rate deals may be on unpopular models that can't be sold without an incentive.

Before going for the lowest rates, do your research and find a vehicle with high ratings from an independent source.

"It may make better sense over the long term to buy a consistently reliable model at a little higher interest than an unreliable model at zero per cent," says *Consumer Reports* magazine.

Negotiate a deal without saying whether you're paying cash or financing the purchase. "Simply say you haven't decided," says Phil Edmonston, author of the *Lemon-Aid* car buying guides. "Once you have a fair price, then take advantage of the financing or rebate program."

The car you want may come with an ultra-low financing rate or a cash rebate. What's a better deal? How do you choose?

Zero-interest financing may be more attractive to repeat buyers or those whose credit is squeaky clean. But first-time buyers and those whose credit rating isn't great are better off taking the cash rebate.

Everyone is eligible for rebates, but that's not always true for discount financing. If you don't have a lot of cash or another car to trade in, you should use the cash rebate to reduce your down payment.

Meanwhile, don't let up on your negotiating. "The rebate comes directly from the manufacturer," says *Consumer Reports* at its Web site (www.consumerreports.org), "so there's no reason why you shouldn't get the dealer's best price and the rebate, too."

Popular models that are in short supply are less likely to come with rebates—and they are less likely to allow for negotiating.

What does this suggest to the savvy consumer? If you've seen ads screaming about incentives on certain models of cars or trucks, try to negotiate even deeper discounts. Chances are the manufacturer has overproduced or undersold and has too many on hand.

"A rebate is the signal there may be even more flexibility on the price," says *Consumer Reports*.

Also, don't fall in love with a particular car. By staying flexible, you're more likely to end up with a car you like at a price you'll love.

Don't think car leasing is cheaper

Leasing is no bargain compared to buying a car with a regular loan. In fact, leasing is often more expensive. The disclosure rules are weak and dealers can bundle in extra costs that consumers don't recognize. And the tax benefits of leasing over conventional financing disappeared when Ottawa changed the tax rules in 1991. There's only one reason why many drivers think leasing is the way to go: Lower monthly payments.

"Leases and loans are simply two different methods of automobile financing," says Leaseguide.com, an independent Web site with a wealth of information for consumers. "One finances the use of a vehicle; the other finances the purchase of a vehicle."

When you buy, you pay for the entire cost of the car, regardless of how many kilometres you drive it. When you lease, you pay for only a portion of the vehicle's cost. That's the part you "use up" during the time you're driving it.

Suppose you lease a car that costs $20,000, but is worth only $13,000 after two years. You pay for the $7,000 difference (known as depreciation), plus finance charges and fees. When you buy, you pay the entire $20,000, plus finance charges.

Since you pay only for what you use, your monthly lease payments are 30 to 60 per cent lower than for a purchase loan of the same term. This is true even with a zero per cent loan.

Here are other benefits of leasing that dealers like to pitch:

- Your monthly payments are lower, so you can get more car for the same money and drive a brand-new vehicle every two to four years, depending on the length of your lease.

- Your lease can be the same length as the manufacturer's warranty, so if something major goes wrong with the car it's always covered.

- You have a lower up-front cash outlay, since most leases require little or no down payment. This frees up your cash for other things.

- You pay less sales tax, because you're taxed only on the portion of the value you use during your lease. The tax isn't paid up front (as with buying), but is spread out and paid along with your monthly lease payment.

- If you own your own business or work for yourself, you can write off the portion of the cost of leasing applicable to your work.

- You don't have the hassle of selling a used car later. You simply turn back your car to the leasing company when your lease ends, unless you decide to buy it or trade it.

While leasing is cheaper in the short term, it won't save you money overall. In the medium term, leasing costs about the same as buying, assuming you sell your car at the end of the loan. Most people don't. This also assumes you wisely invest your monthly lease savings, instead of using them to buy groceries and cover household expenses. In the long term, leasing always costs more than buying if you keep your vehicle. As you continue driving the car over many years, you spread the cost over a longer term.

"It doesn't take rocket science to figure out that the cost of buying one car and driving it for 10 years is less expensive than leasing five different cars over the same period," says Leaseguide.com.

If long-term financial benefits are important to you, then you should always choose to buy and keep the car for many years. With so much quality built into today's cars—the average vehicle goes to the junkyard with 250,000 kilometres on it—why opt for a lease that lasts two to three years?

"If you like to own your car for more than five years, then don't lease," says Dennis DesRosiers, who heads his own automotive consulting firm in Toronto. "Over a lifetime of car ownership, leasing is the most expensive way to go."

While leasing offers lower payments, you have nothing at the end. You can buy the car outright, lease another one or walk away. To avoid high repair costs, most people turn in the old leased car and lease a shiny new vehicle with a new manufacturer's warranty.

A lease is a monthly payment for life. Wouldn't you rather have a monthly payment for a limited time? When you take out a loan, you pay off the car in a few years and drive payment-free afterward.

"Leasing encourages you to get more product than you can afford and do it more often. To me, leasing plays to all the things in your psychology that say, me, more, now," says DesRosiers.

Here are some disadvantages of leasing:

- The maintenance guidelines are quite strict. You're responsible for excess wear and tear, which is usually spelled out in the contract. This means you may have to pay extra charges to cover paint chips, scratches and tire wear. Do the repairs yourself before returning the car.

- The mileage is limited. Most leases allow you to drive 24,000 kilometres a year, but some give only 18,000. You may be charged 8 to 15 cents a kilometre once you exceed the quota. If you drive a lot, try to negotiate a lower excess mileage charge up front.

- Lease contracts can be difficult to understand. Moreover, they're surprisingly prone to mistakes. You must be able to catch and correct these problems before you sign the contract. Afterward it's too late.

It's important that you read your contract and be able to verify the monthly payment figures yourself, before signing.

If the math confuses you, a $35 piece of software can take the mystery out of leasing. Rob Lo Presti developed the Car Calculator program in 1993 to help people decipher lease contracts. It's not sold in stores, but can be ordered at www.b4usign.com or by telephone (1-877-248-7446).

The Canadian Financing and Leasing Association offers a free booklet, "Turning the Lights on Leasing," with a straightforward explanation of the things you need to know. Check the Web site (www.cfla-acfl.ca) and click on Industry Info, or call (416) 860-1133 or toll-free, 1-877-213-7373.

Watch out for car lease penalties

You can get into trouble if you have to give up your leased car before the lease term is up. If you lose your job, you may be stuck with a car you don't want and can't afford to keep. But walking away can be even more costly. A *Toronto Star* reader had an awful experience with a leased car. His story is an example of what not to do.

Jim leased a car for business purposes. His company paid the $750-a-month lease cost, plus gas and insurance. When he lost his job about halfway through the lease, he returned the car to the dealer. He left instructions to contact his former employer.

Two months later, Jim got a disturbing call from General Motors Acceptance Corp., which had financed his Chevy Blazer. He was told that he was considered the lessee of the vehicle, not his employer. As such, he'd have to pay $11,300 for prematurely terminating the lease.

Never assume the employer is leasing the car, even if the company is making the payments. If you sign the lease, you're on the hook. And don't think you can return the car to the dealer in mid-lease without consequences. The finance company considers you are terminating the lease. It sells the car for whatever price it can get and deducts the proceeds from what you owe.

Jim insists he simply parked the car at the dealer, while waiting to see what his employer decided to do with it. "Once GMAC decided that I in fact was the lessee, it should have contacted me immediately," he told me.

But a GMAC executive said there is no time to notify everyone individually. "Unfortunately, we get way too many of these things happening to pick up the phone and call the customer to ask, 'Do you know what you're doing?'"

Returning a car to a dealer before the lease is up is considered a voluntary surrender. This allows the finance company to sell the vehicle through a public auction and bill you for any shortfall.

Jim says he would have continued making the payments for the remaining 18 months. He asked about this option when GMAC called him two months later. By then, it was too late. The car had been sold.

I asked leasing expert Rob Lo Presti about this case. He said GMAC and the dealer should have explained to Jim what would happen if he returned the vehicle early and estimated what it would cost him to terminate the lease.

Once Jim knew the cost of termination, he could have compared it to other options. These would have included:

- Continue leasing until the term was up. This would have cost him $13,558, but he would have kept the car.

- Buy the vehicle, sell it and pay off the outstanding amount. This would have put him, not the leasing company, in control of the sale.

- Advertise for strangers to take over the lease. But Jim could still be on the hook if the person who took over the lease defaulted on the payments.

Jim had an additional reason to be angry. GMAC wouldn't disclose the price his car fetched at the auction, nor would it break down the costs involved in the $11,300 termination fee.

If you lose your job and can't keep up your car lease, take time to consider your options. Think carefully about Jim's experience before you let the leasing company sell the car on your behalf.

Luckily, there's an insurance policy that protects you from financial losses when you cut short your lease. The Walkaway Protection Plan, underwritten by ING Wellington Insurance Co., is offered by a number of car dealers in Canada. The plan is free for the first year, after which you pay the cost yourself if you want coverage.

For a $199 premium, you're covered for up to $7,500 in losses if you have to end a lease or loan early for the following reasons:

- You're laid off from your job.

- You're transferred overseas.

- You lose your driver's license.

- You become disabled or critically ill.

- You go personally bankrupt if you're self-employed.

Customers have walked away from $2.6 million in loan and lease obligations since the plan began in January 2000, the company says at its Web site (www.walkawayprotection.com).

As with most insurance policies, there are a few conditions. But they're not onerous (and no medical exams are required). You must have made at least two payments on the vehicle. You can't make a claim if you're downsized or transferred overseas within the first three months. And if you've lost your job, you must be collecting employment insurance. There are no age restrictions on the free one-year coverage. But those who buy a full-term policy must be under age 79 at the time of purchase.

If you need to terminate early, you can find companies that specialize in lease transfers. They match people who want to get out of a lease with others who are looking for bargain short-term leases on late-model, low-mileage vehicles. Make sure your lease company allows such transfers.

You also need to get a type of insurance called gap protection. This protects you from being personally liable if your leased car is stolen or totally destroyed. It covers any additional amount you might owe after your insurance company pays off.

Your insurance company gives you only what the car is worth. If you're "upside down" (owing more on your lease than the car's value), the insurance will come up short. That's why you need extra coverage. Find out if gap protection is included in your lease contract or included for a fee. If there are no gap provisions at all, it's available from independent sources.

Read the fine print in your contract to see what protection you already have and what you need. If you can't understand the contract, contact an independent expert.

Take out your wallet and open it up. Count up the credit cards you're carrying. I don't mean the gasoline or department store cards, but the number of Visa and MasterCard credit cards you have. Here's the number you need: One or two. Anything more and you're paying too much in annual fees and interest costs.

"This isn't just an exercise in keeping a neat purse or wallet," says Gordon Pape in *Six Steps to $1 Million* (Prentice Hall Canada). "If you're a normal credit card user, you can probably save yourself hundreds of dollars each year by applying some basic financial management disciplines."

To decide which cards to keep, spread them out on the table. Now get rid of those you've used fewer than four times over the past year. Pay off the balances on those cards and cancel them with the issuers.

Credit card marketers are clever people. They're always introducing new cards with new features and urging you to apply. Sometimes they say you're "pre-approved" for a card because you're such a good customer. Free flights and travel are just some of the goodies you can get for everyday shopping. With the right card, you can earn free toys (Citibank's Sony MasterCard), transportation (TD Canada

Trust's GM card and Harley-Davidson Visa) and tools (Canadian Tire Options MasterCard). There's even a card that contributes to a retirement plan for you or an education plan for your kids (MBNA Equity MasterCard). "Book a vacation or shop at your favourite store and know that you're building a nest egg with each purchase," says MBNA. Spending your way to security: Now there's an idea.

Affinity cards are the newest growth area. Instead of rewards, you can donate a share of your purchases to a good cause. Feel virtuous about supporting a favourite charity, university or sporting group— and it doesn't cost you a penny.

Before you know it, you're carrying half a dozen credit cards. Many have annual fees and most have interest rates that are stuck in the 18 to 20 per cent range, no matter how low the prime rate goes. And while you intend to pay off the balance each month, there may be times when you spend more with your multiple cards than you can comfortably handle.

You're not alone. There are 44 million Visa and MasterCard cards circulating in Canada. Surveys show 50 per cent of cardholders don't pay their bills in full or on time. More than 40 per cent of cardholders say they don't know the interest rate on their cards, according to a Leger survey in December 2001. Suppose you carry a $1,000 balance from month to month. That costs you $180 in interest a year if you have a card with no annual fee and an 18 per cent interest rate. But many cards do have annual fees, especially the gold cards with the enticing travel rewards. You'll be astounded at what you pay once you factor in the fees. Here are some examples:

- CIBC Aerogold Visa has a $120 fee and a 19.5 per cent rate. The cost of carrying a $1,000 balance is $315 a year. That's an annual rate of 31.5 per cent.

- Royal Bank Avion Gold Visa has a $120 fee and an 18.5 per cent rate. The cost of carrying a $1,000 balance is $305 a year, or 30.5 per cent.

- TD Canada Trust has a Gold Travel Visa with a $99 fee and an 18.5 per cent rate. The cost of carrying a $1,000 balance is $284 a year, or 28.4 per cent.

- Bank of Montreal has a Gold MasterCard with Air Miles, which has a $95 fee and an 18.4 per cent rate. The cost of carrying a $1,000 balance is $279, or 27.9 per cent.

You can do your own math with credit card calculators. I used one at the Web site of *Money Sense* magazine, www.moneysense.ca.

You're fooling yourself when you slice and dice your debt onto several cards. Better to have everything in one place, so you know exactly what you owe. You know the expression "Don't put all your eggs in one basket." That makes sense for your investments, which are too risky if they're not diversified. But when it comes to credit cards, you *should* have all your eggs in one basket. You'll have an easier time monitoring your indebtedness and not letting it get out of control.

Here are some signs of credit card trouble:

- You're making only the minimum payments on your accounts.

- You're missing payments or due dates.

- You're near the credit limit on most of your cards.

- You're borrowing from one card to pay another.

- You don't know (or want to know) how much money you owe.

- You worry a lot about money.

- You use credit cards to meet your weekly or monthly living expenses.

- You transfer balances from one low-rate card to another every few months, just before the introductory offer expires.

It's time to address your financial problems if you recognize some of these patterns in your own life. Here's a six-step program from a Toronto bankruptcy trustee, Frank Kisluk.

1. Be honest with yourself. Do a complete analysis of all your debts, the interest rates and terms.

2. Decide how much money you can use to pay off debt each month.

3. If there's a shortfall, consider getting a consolidation loan or line of credit at a lower rate.

4. Consider selling investments to pay off high-rate debt. If you own a house, bump up your mortgage at renewal time.

5. Pay the minimum amount on each card. Use what's left to pay off the card with the highest rate.

6. Don't use the cards any more. Cut them up or put them into a box.

Buying everything with cash, cheques or no-overdraft debit cards forces you to confront the fact you can't afford something, Kisluk says. "With a credit card, you can always afford it."

Pick the right card for your needs

Choosing a credit card is no easy matter. Ignore the many offers that arrive in the mail or come from your financial institution. A credit card may be wrong for you, despite the fact you're pre-approved and highly desired as a customer.

Spend a little time comparing the features of each card. You can't check out all of them, since there are just too many. More than 600 institutions in Canada put out credit cards through 19 principal issuers, including banks, credit unions and retailers. Our credit card market is one of the most competitive in the world.

There are four major categories of cards:

- **Standard credit cards**. They charge a high interest rate on outstanding balances and often have loyalty programs.

- **Low-rate cards**. They have lower interest rates than standard cards, but most charge an annual fee.

- **Retail cards**. They charge a higher interest rate than standard cards, but there's no annual fee. The issuing retailer may offer rewards.

■ **Charge cards**. They charge high penalties for those who don't pay off their entire balances each month. There's an annual fee and often a high credit limit.

The Financial Consumer Agency of Canada puts out a quarterly report, "Credit Cards and You," that compares rates, fees and other features on many cards. The current report and the back copies are posted at www.fcac-acfc.gc.ca. You can also find these reports at Industry Canada's Web site, www.strategis.gc.ca. What you won't find, unfortunately, is a comparison of gold and platinum cards. The FCAC, a federal government agency, has decided that customers who want these prestige cards can do their own legwork.

The credit card comparison tables often show several rates. Many cards have one rate for purchases and another for cash advances. (A cash advance occurs when you use the credit card to borrow money or to pay a bill.) Often, there's another rate for balance transfers. (A balance transfer is when you move an existing debt from one credit card to another to take advantage of lower rates.)

If you choose a card with a low introductory rate, always find out what rate you'll pay when the special offer ends. Don't settle for a range of rates. Find out what your rate will be, based on your credit score. Capital One, for example, aggressively promotes a card with a zero introductory rate for the first six months. Customers pay 9.9 to 19.9 per cent after a few months. That's too big a range. Ask where you fit on the sliding scale. Also, ask whether the introductory rate period will suddenly come to an end if you make a late payment or exceed your credit limit.

Be careful when moving your balance to a card with a low introductory rate. The low rate generally applies only to the transferred amount. You'll pay a higher rate for new purchases charged to the card and cash advances. So put the new card away and don't use it until you've paid off your balance.

Here are two reasons to limit card use for new purchases when you transfer a balance:

- There's no interest-free period on new purchases. You begin paying interest at the card's higher rate on new purchases from the date you make them or (in some cases) the day they're posted to your account.

- Card issuers apply your payments to balance transfers and cash advances before applying them to new purchases. This means you're paying the lower-interest debt first and carrying the higher-interest debt (from purchases) for a longer time.

Some card issuers apply your payments in a different order. Don't hesitate to ask if you're not sure.

The Financial Consumer Agency gives an example of how you can pay higher interest when you transfer a balance and use a card for new purchases. Suppose your balance is $5,000. You move it to a new card with a 6 per cent introductory rate for balance transfers and an 18 per cent rate for purchases. Your payments are applied first to balance transfers, then to purchases.

In the first case, you make no other purchases during the month. You pay $25.47 in interest charges on the balance transfer at the end of the month.

In the second case, you make a purchase of $1,000 with the new card a few days after you get it. The following day, you make a partial payment of $1,000 to bring your balance back to $5,000. You think you're back to square one, but you're not. You pay $34.53 in interest charges, $9.06 more than in the first case. That's because your $1,000 purchase was outstanding for 27 days of the month, not one day as you assumed.

A low-rate credit card is your best bet if you carry a balance each month. Did you know that most financial institutions have a low-rate card? They're not as widely advertised as the higher-priced cards with the goodies.

Even though most low-rate cards carry an annual fee, you'll probably still save money because of the lower interest costs. To see how much you can save in total borrowing costs, check out the credit card costs calculator at Industry Canada's Web site, www.strategis.gc.ca. (Click C for Credit Card.)

Suppose you carry a $1,500 balance and you never take any cash advances. Among the big banks, the Bank of Nova Scotia's Value Visa offers the best deal with a 9.9 per cent annual interest rate and a $29 annual fee. That works out to the equivalent of 11.83 per cent a year. Your total cost is $177.50.

Not everyone likes paying fees for credit cards, so Scotiabank has another low-rate card. The No-Fee Value Visa has an interest rate of 11.9 per cent a year, slightly more than the Value Visa's 11.83 per cent. With your $1,500 balance, your total cost is $178.50 a year (just $1 more).

Royal Bank has the second-best deal. Its Visa Classic low-rate card has a 10.5 per cent interest rate and a $25 annual fee. That works out to an adjusted rate of 12.17 per cent. Your total cost to carry a $1,500 balance for a year is $182.50.

How much do you save with a low-rate card? That's easy to find out. The credit card costs calculator does the math for you.

If you used Scotiabank's no-fee standard card with an 18.5 per cent interest rate, you would pay $277.50 to carry a $1,500 balance for a year. So you save $100 a year with the Value Visa. (This assumes you carry a constant balance and you make all minimum payments on time.)

You save $86 a year with Royal Bank's Classic Visa low-rate card. If you used the no-fee standard card with a 17.9 per cent interest rate, you would pay $268.50 to carry a $1,500 balance.

When shopping for a credit card, check the grace period—the time between the statement date and the payment due date. You pay no interest during the grace period.

The grace period is a less important consideration if you have an outstanding balance. The interest clock starts ticking on the date the transaction is posted to your account.

Among low-rate cards, Scotiabank's Value Visa cards have the longest grace period—26 days. The CIBC's Select Visa low-rate card offers 24 days, but the Bank of Montreal's low-rate MasterCard gives only 19 days.

If you have trouble paying what you owe each month, stay away from charge cards such as American Express and Diners Club. The balance is payable in full by the due date and usually can't be rolled over to the next month. Late payments are hit with a punitive 30 per cent interest rate. "In addition, if you pay late, your account may be temporarily frozen or your card revoked," the Financial Consumer Agency points out.

Avoid retail cards, too, if you don't pay on time. Sears, HBC (Hudson's Bay and Zellers) and Canadian Tire charge 28.8 per cent a year, a rate that hasn't budged for decades. However, these retailers provide a generous grace period of 25 to 30 days and calculate interest from the statement date.

Petro-Canada charges 24 per cent a year and calculates interest from the purchase date. This is a less generous method than calculating interest from the statement date.

Suppose you make a purchase on June 18. If you pay with a Visa or MasterCard, the interest is charged from either June 18 or the date your transaction is posted at the bank (June 19 or 20). But if you pay with a Sears or HBC card, the interest will be charged from the date your monthly bill is prepared (as late as July 15).

Find out how interest is calculated

If you don't pay your credit card bill on time, you will be charged interest. That's no surprise. But the way the interest is calculated can come as a great surprise, especially if you've paid off most of the balance.

Jim, a *Toronto Star* reader, had a $2,660.11 balance on a Royal Bank Visa Gold card. He paid off $2,478.40 in one month, leaving just $181.71 unpaid. The interest charge was $35.72, almost 20 per cent of the outstanding balance. "We were not prepared for a charge this large on such a small amount," he said in a letter to the Royal Bank of Canada's ombudsman.

You probably don't know about this calculation quirk unless you've experienced it. Many Visa and MasterCard issuers charge interest on the whole amount—not just the amount outstanding—if the balance is not paid in full.

Jim read his cardholder agreement over and found it didn't state clearly that he would be charged interest on money the bank had already received. Later, he checked the Canadian Imperial Bank of Commerce's Visa cardholder agreement and found it did a better job of explaining the rules.

Jim didn't get anywhere with his complaint, but I later heard from another reader, Raymond, who had some interest charges reversed when he complained. He was a long-time American Express Air Miles cardholder with a strong payment record, and the company didn't want to lose him. Raymond's experience shows you can get concessions when you complain, if you're a good customer.

You may be charged interest on the whole amount, not just the unpaid balance, even if you make a mistake and pay off all but 50 cents or $1 of your bill. So examine your cheques carefully to avoid errors.

Suppose you return an item bought with a credit card and the refund hasn't yet appeared on your statement. It makes sense to pay the full amount that appears on the statement. If you apply the credit yourself, you will have an outstanding balance and face a high interest charge. The same goes if you dispute a credit-card charge. Pay first and then argue.

Card issuers have two different ways of deciding whether the interest-free period applies to your new purchases. The Financial Consumer Agency distinguishes between them in its quarterly cost comparison tables. Mr. Jones, for example, doesn't pay his balance in full in May. He carries over $1,000 into June and also makes a $3,000 purchase during the month. He pays the $4,000 balance in full by the due date.

If the card issuer uses the first method, Mr. Jones has to pay interest only on the $1,000 carried over from May. But with the second method, Mr. Jones has to pay interest on the $1,000 balance carried over from May *and* on the new $3,000 purchase in June if he fails to pay his May balance in full.

Read your credit card agreement, or check with the issuer, to see which method it uses. American Express, Citibank, Capital One and MBNA use the less generous method of calculating interest-free periods for their standard cards, according to the Financial Consumer Agency.

Remember that there's no grace period for cash advances. Interest is calculated from the day you borrow the money. Pay off the cash advance as soon as possible. Don't wait until you get your monthly statement.

Many credit card issuers charge different rates for cash advances and for purchases. If you regularly borrow money with your credit card, find out what the true rate is. And if you use cash advances as a constant source of financing, look at cheaper alternatives, like a personal line of credit.

Premium cards offer attractive rewards. If you charge enough purchases to the card, you can get free travel and merchandise—even discounts on cars (with the GM Card from TD Canada Trust or Citibank's Driver's Edge). You can also opt to get cash rebates on what you spend.

Remember, however, that rewards can be cut off at any time. Loyal customers get furious, but there's nothing they can do. Card issuers put fine print in their agreements letting them change or cancel the loyalty programs if they're not profitable.

Among the examples:

■ Ford Motor Co. of Canada cancelled a credit card, co-sponsored with CIBC, with discounts on new Ford vehicles. Many cardholders weren't able to buy a new car before the program was cut off. And Ford didn't allow using the points for other purchases, such as repairs at Ford dealerships.

■ General Motors of Canada changed its GM Card program. Customers used to collect five per cent on purchases, with discounts up to $3,500 on any new GM vehicle. Starting Jan. 1, 2003, they get only three per cent on purchases and lower discounts. The $3,500 rebate is for only higher-end Cadillac models.

■ Air Miles revamped its flight rewards, basing them not on distance but on a zone system. Customers who had saved enough points to fly to a destination found they needed to save more.

Card loyalty programs can disappear tomorrow and there's no consumer protection. So if you're collecting points, use them quickly or you may lose them.

But premium cards can be worth their annual fees. They offer attractive benefits like travel health insurance, rental car collision insurance and purchase protection. These insurance perks are worth a bundle if you have to make a claim.

Check the benefits to see which ones you can use. Travel medical insurance is great if you take lots of trips, but you may rarely leave home. Or you may already have this insurance as part of an employee benefits package. Older people, those over 65 or 70, usually don't qualify for coverage.

A collision damage waiver covers the cost of repairs to a rented vehicle over and above the deductible if you have an accident. Car rental companies charge $10 to $15 a day for this protection. But if you hardly ever rent cars, this isn't a benefit you need.

With purchase protection, you're covered for the cost of any merchandise you buy with the card if it's lost, stolen or damaged in the first few months. Anyone can use this type of insurance. For example, a member of my ski club used it to replace his brand-new skis, which were stolen on his first trip to Europe. He'd paid more than $1,000 for them.

Premium cardholders often don't recognize how powerful their purchase protection is. For example, it covers services as well as goods. Suppose your fitness club goes out of business a few months after you paid $500 for a one-year membership. If you charged the cost to the credit card, you may be covered for what you lost.

Jeannette, a *Toronto Star* reader, didn't know she could claim for purchase protection. She had given a $1,000 credit card deposit for laser eye surgery, a procedure not covered by provincial health insurance. She later changed her mind and was promised a refund. But the laser surgery firm went bankrupt before she got her money back. A rival firm, hoping to build traffic, said it would honour the bankrupt firm's deposits. But Jeannette, a nurse, got cold feet about laser eye surgery after reading about the risks. She didn't want the procedure done elsewhere. She just wanted her money back.

"Did you check with your credit card issuer?" I asked. Jeannette had paid with a Scotiabank Platinum Visa card, which provides purchase protection for 180 days. "No, I never considered it," she replied. She made a claim just in time, 174 days after giving her deposit, and found she was indeed covered. The refund came promptly.

Shop around to see what benefits you get with a premium card. Make a list of what's important to you. If you want purchase protection, check the coverage period. Some cards offer six months, some three months. Extended warranty protection, a related benefit, covers product defects that crop up after the manufacturer's warranty ends. It, too, can save you big money if something goes wrong.

Each premium card offers a different combination of benefits. You can't assume that the most expensive cards have the best perks. For example, CIBC offers purchase security insurance and extended warranty coverage on its $99 Gold Visa card, $79 Dividend Platinum card and free Dividend card—but not on the $120 Aerogold Visa card.

Once you pick a premium card, review the benefits so you're familiar with them. Read the contracts closely and check for coverage limits and exclusions. Then use the benefits as much as you can. They're part of the package you're paying for and represent a big chunk of your annual fees.

Monitor your use of the premium card regularly to see whether it's the right product for your needs. If not, shop around and find something better. Apply for a low-rate card if you can't pay off your monthly bills and use it for most of your spending (even if it means giving up some reward points). Keep the premium card if you want the insurance benefits, but try not to rack up a high balance.

Preserve your good credit rating

Credit cards are convenient, since you can pay for purchases without carrying cash. And with the grace period, you have up to six weeks before you have to send in your money. You can use your credit card to order tickets over the telephone, book a flight, rent a car or reserve a hotel room. A card is your passport to the world of electronic commerce. Without one, you're grounded.

Treat your credit cards with respect. Use them carefully or you could lose them.

Here are ways to avoid credit card abuse:

- Pay as much as you can each month. Don't pay just the minimum amount. The minimum is enough to keep your account in good standing, but it's not enough to make a dent in your debt.

- Stay below your credit limit. If you exceed the limit, the card issuer may just give you a higher limit. But your credit rating will suffer.

- Stick with one or two cards. If you carry a balance, don't keep applying for new cards with higher limits or lower rates. You can switch from one card to another, but make sure to cancel the old card.

- Contact the card issuer if you can't make a payment. Don't miss more than two months in a row.

It's tempting to pay just the minimum amount when bills pile up. You can do it once in a while, but you'll get into trouble if you do it every month. By paying only the minimum, you will extend the repayment period for many extra months. And that will raise the cost of your credit card purchase. It could double the cost.

Suppose you buy a leather jacket for $1,000 and put it on a credit card with an 18.5 per cent annual rate. You have no other debts and you pay the minimum, say three per cent of the balance each month.

At that rate, you will take more than ten years (122 months) to pay off the balance, and your total interest paid will be $842.90. That $1,000 leather jacket will end up costing you $1,842.90.

If the minimum is only two per cent, you'll take more than 20 years (248 months) to discharge the debt. You will pay $2,144.83 in interest, thus tripling the cost of your purchase.

Credit card companies don't want you to know this. They're happy to let you keep paying the minimum. But it's dangerous to your financial health, as you can see from the above examples. (I worked them out using a credit calculator at www.cardweb.com, a U.S. Web site that keeps a close eye on rates and trends.)

There are two ways to reduce interest costs on your purchase of the $1,000 leather jacket: Pay off more of the balance each month or switch to a lower-rate card.

If you pay 10 per cent of the monthly balance, you'll discharge the debt in 37 months with an interest cost of $173.48. And if you pay a fixed amount of $100 a month, you'll whittle that down to ten months and $84.79 in interest.

Now look what happens when you switch to a credit card with a 10.5 per cent interest rate. By paying a flat $100 a month, you'll be debt-free in ten months at an interest cost of $48.12. A low-rate card saves you money even if you pay just the minimum. If you use a card with a 10.5 per cent rate and pay three per cent of the monthly balance, you'll get rid of the debt in 91 months with an interest cost of $337. That's a considerable improvement from the 122-month repayment period and $842.90 interest cost when you use a standard card with an 18.5 per cent interest rate.

Your credit rating will suffer if you have too much debt and you're paying only the minimum amount, or your credit card balances are close to the limit. It's worth checking your credit report periodically to see how you're doing.

Check out your credit report

Every year or two, you should get a copy of your credit report. This is a history of how consistently you pay your obligations to companies that lend money or issue credit cards to you (banks, credit unions, retailers and finance companies).

Credit reporting agencies, also known as credit bureaus, are private institutions that supply information to credit granters. If you find any mistakes, you can ask the credit bureau to make the correction at no charge.

There may be wrong or outdated information on your file, such as a payment you made that isn't reflected or a loan you already paid off. Occasionally, one person gets mixed up with someone else and acquires a whole new history. This can happen if you have a common name or relatives with similar names.

Credit bureaus make errors and so do the credit granters that supply their information. You won't automatically hear about problems with your credit report. Your only clue will be if you apply for a loan or a new credit card and you're turned down.

To get your credit report from Canada's two big credit bureaus, you have to make a request in writing. (You can't do it by telephone.)

Send a letter or download an application from their Web sites.

Here are details on the credit agencies:

- Equifax Canada Inc. Write to: National Consumer Relations, P.O. Box 190, Station Jean-Talon, Montreal, Quebec H1S 2Z2. Telephone 1-800-465-7166. Web site www.equifax.ca.

- TransUnion Canada. Write to: Consumer Relations Centre, P.O. Box 338, LCD 1, Hamilton, Ont. L8L 7W2. Telephone 1-800-663-9980. Web site www.tuc.ca.

Both credit bureaus will ask for two pieces of identification, as well as your birth date and current and previous addresses. You don't have to give your social insurance number (SIN). You will receive your credit report in the mail in a couple of weeks.

The report lists the credit cards and loans in your name. Mortgage information is not yet included, but will be coming soon. You can see the credit limits on each account, your current balance and payment history (whether and how often you pay 30, 60 or 90 days late).

Any information that affects your creditworthiness—a recent personal bankruptcy or an account turned over to a collection agency—will be there.

Suppose you've been turned down for a loan or credit card. You're desperate to get funds and you want to see something quickly. Equifax Canada provides immediate online access to your credit report for a fee. You pay with a credit card at www.econsumer.equifax.ca.

A basic credit report costs $14.50 (no tax). An expanded report, which includes a credit score, costs $21.95. You can see how you compare to other Canadians on a scale of 300 to 900. The higher your score, the more favourably lenders look at you as a credit risk.

If you have a lower-than-average score, you will find out what brought it down. There may be an overdue bill that went for collection, a number of late payments or too much owed on the accounts. You will also get tips on how to improve your credit standing.

Here's a report on a fictitious customer, Jane Doe, who has a credit score of 701:

- She's in a group with 19 per cent of the population who have a credit score of 700 to 749. More than half of Canadians (56 per cent) have a score above 750. The average is 770.

- Her group has a loan delinquency rate of five per cent. That means for every 100 borrowers in this range, approximately five will default on a loan, apply for bankruptcy or fall 90 days past due on at least one credit account in the next two years.

- Her score is lower than average because she has a relatively high number of accounts with balances and the proportion of balances to credit limits is too high.

- She is considered an acceptable risk by most lenders and would be offered competitive terms and rates on loan products.

"It is important to understand that different lenders set their own policies and tolerance for risk when making credit decisions," Equifax explains, "so there is no single 'cut-off' score used by all lenders."

Besides your credit score, lenders look at other factors. They will take into account the security (if any) for your loan and the relationship they have with you, which may include other financial services.

To improve your credit score, don't run up your balances to the limit. Keeping your account balances below 75 per cent of your available credit may help your score, Equifax advises. Avoid applying for credit unless you have a genuine need for a new account. Too many inquiries from credit granters in a short period of time can be a sign that you have financial problems or you're overextending yourself by taking on more debt than you can repay.

Every province except New Brunswick has consumer credit reporting legislation that gives you the right to find out what is in your file. When you make a request, a credit bureau must make the information in your file available to you and list all the companies that have requested it lately.

You can dispute inaccurate information by submitting any evidence that supports your claim. The credit bureau will investigate and advise you of its results. If the investigation doesn't resolve the dispute, you can add a brief statement to your file. The credit bureau will include a summary of your statement in future reports.

Stay away from "credit repair" services. These companies, which charge $1,000 or more, run classified advertisements saying they can remove negative information from your credit files. But they can't do anything more than you can do yourself.

Ontario has amended its credit reporting law to better regulate these services. Credit repair firms have to say in their contracts that consumers have the legal right to review a credit file and dispute any inaccurate information. Instead of charging for the full amount up front, these companies have to wait till they make a material change in someone's credit file.

Protect yourself
from identity theft

It's bad enough when thieves grab your wallet or purse. They can ring up big charges on your credit cards before you even notice something is missing. Generally, though, you're not responsible for any unauthorized charges if you notify the credit granters promptly.

Identity theft is more insidious. Instead of stealing your plastic, thieves hack into computers to get confidential information about you or intercept letters sent in the mail to your home. It's one of the fastest-growing types of crime.

Fraud artists use your personal details to open credit card accounts in your name. Sometimes they take over an existing account and redirect the mail to a new address. Unless you watch carefully, you may not notice that you have missed a monthly bill or two.

To protect yourself, you should guard your identifying documents as if they were gold or treasure. They are indeed valuable, worth thousands of dollars in the wrong hands. Don't make it easy for criminals to get everything in one fell swoop.

Here are a few ways to foil identity thieves:

- Keep your social insurance card in a safe place at home. Don't carry it around in your wallet. If the card is stolen, notify the local office of Human Resources Development Canada right away.

- If your driver's license is lost or stolen, contact your local vehicle license issuing office and the police immediately.

- If your chequebook is lost or stolen, let the bank know. Mention which cheque numbers are missing.

- Keep your chequebook separate from your credit cards.

- Don't give your credit card number over the telephone unless you know it's a reputable company and you have initiated the call. Avoid saying the numbers loud enough so that others around you can hear.

- Store monthly credit card statements safely. Check them against your receipts to make sure there are no unauthorized purchases.

- If you receive a letter saying you're pre-authorized for credit, destroy it before throwing it out. Get into the habit of shredding sensitive papers you want to discard.

- Memorize all passwords and personal identification numbers, so you don't have to write them down.

- Notify Canada Post if you discover your credit card statements have not been delivered, but the sender confirms they were sent.

- If you order a confidential credit report by mail, notify the credit bureau if it doesn't arrive.

You should suspect you're a fraud victim if you find out about a credit application in your name, but you didn't send in that application. You may get calls from a collection agency trying to get money on a defaulted account that you didn't open.

Contact the credit bureau if you think there's a problem. It will investigate and, if necessary, add a statement to your report that will alert future credit granters to call you and confirm your identify before issuing new credit.

You should have a complete list of your creditors so you can contact them directly. The credit bureau doesn't do this. Keep their toll-free numbers handy. If you can't keep track of the credit cards you carry around, here's an easy way to remember. Take them out of your wallet and photocopy both sides. This will serve as a reference if they're lost or stolen. The toll-free number is usually printed on the card. Don't worry about calling after hours. Most credit card companies operate call centres that stay open 24 hours a day, seven days a week, for theft and fraud complaints.

part three

Saving for Retirement

You may be tempted to skip this section. Don't do it, even if you're under 40 and retirement is the last thing on your mind. A little planning won't hurt.

Don't skip this section, either, if you're over 40 and retirement is the last thing on your mind. RRSP advertisers try to make you feel guilty if you don't start saving by the age of 20. Procrastinators shouldn't lose hope. It's never too late to start.

Here's why I want you to think about retirement. Chances are you'll leave work earlier and live longer than your parents or grandparents. How will you support yourself for 20, 30 or 40 years after you stop getting a regular paycheque?

Government pensions will replace less than half of your income. That's not a lot. It can come as a shock to see how little they cover. And with governments under pressure to cut back benefits, you may have to wait till you're older to collect, or you may pay back more in taxes.

Employer pensions can help fill the gap. But what you get depends on where you work and how long you stay. If you're lucky, you'll spend your career in a public sector job and retire with a generous pension that's tied to the cost of living. More likely, you'll work in the private sector and retire with a modest pension that shrinks each year as inflation rises.

That's why most of us need to save on our own. We can't rely on government and employer pensions to finance the lifestyle we had before retirement. Our savings could make the difference between living in comfort and living in deprivation.

Many people aged 45 to 64 haven't saved enough for retirement. About 30 per cent of families and 46 per cent of singles won't have enough assets to replace two-thirds of their pre-retirement incomes, according to Statistics Canada. Moreover, 59 per cent of those who don't own a home may not have saved enough.

The sooner you start to save for retirement, the less you need to set aside each year. Young savers do well, but so do those who devote themselves to paying off their mortgage and then saving for retirement. The key is to have a plan.

In this section, we'll look at who needs an RRSP and who doesn't. With their tax advantages, RRSPs are "the closest thing to a personal money machine any of us will ever have," says author Gordon Pape. But RRSPs aren't suitable for everyone.

We'll tell you what to expect from government pensions such as Old Age Security and the Canada Pension Plan. And we'll provide questions to ask employers about their pension plans. This is stuff you need to know early on, not just before you retire.

Finally, you may want to hire a financial adviser to develop and implement a retirement plan. So we'll give guidelines for finding good professional help. Hint: Be careful about the advice you hear at a free financial seminar. The speaker may be more concerned with his or her retirement than with yours.

Deal with debt before saving for retirement

What's the best way to save for retirement? Banks and brokers say you should max out your RRSP contributions each year. But they have a vested interest in this strategy because they sell RRSPs. Here's another answer: Become debt-free by your late 40s. Then get to work on retirement saving.

RRSPs are not a priority for middle-income households in the $60,000 to $70,000 a year range. Consider yourself on the right track if you're paying off your mortgage and putting aside money to educate your kids.

"Being debt-free in Canada is a very important thing, and it's not given the attention it deserves," says Malcolm Hamilton, an actuary with Toronto-based Mercer Human Resources Consulting. "If you're in your mid-40s and you have no debt, you've accomplished an enormous amount. It looks like you're not getting anywhere, but most of the hard work is behind you."

Hamilton is known for his radical views in an industry that makes you feel guilty if you don't start a retirement plan in your 20s. He thinks you can wait to contribute and still live comfortably in your older years.

Many experts, such as author Gordon Pape, don't believe in putting off retirement saving. He uses the example of 20-year-old

Tina and 40-year-old Tony. Both contribute $1,000 a year to an RRSP, earning 6 per cent a year compounded, and both retire at 65.

Early starter Tina contributes $45,000 to her RRSP over 45 years. Her plan is worth $225,508 when she retires. Late starter Tony contributes $25,000 over 25 years, but his plan is worth only $58,156 when he retires ($167,000 less).

Compounding gives Tina a profound edge. She starts sooner and has more time for her money to grow. By saving an extra $20,000 from age 25 to 45, she ends up with a nest egg four times bigger than Tony's.

Tina can stay ahead of Tony even if she stops contributing to her RRSP at age 30 and never adds another penny. That shows the power of compound interest over time.

Still, eliminating debt is a priority. "Not owing any money when you begin your retirement will give you a huge advantage," Pape says. Here are three reasons why you shouldn't carry debt into your 60s:

- Interest payments will be a drain on your retirement income. You may have to reduce your standard of living to find the money to service your debts.

- You won't have windfalls, such as an annual bonus at work, to put toward debt reduction.

- Any sharp spike in interest rates will increase your monthly living costs and put an additional strain on your budget.

RRSPs work brilliantly for affluent, heavily taxed Canadians. They get a tax deduction on their contributions and tax-free growth on their savings. Later, they pay a lower tax rate on their withdrawals since their income usually falls in retirement.

But for Canadians with modest incomes, tax rates increase with age. That's because social services for lower-income seniors are income-tested. RRSP income often has the unwanted effect of raising the cost of social services or resulting in benefits that are taxed back.

"When low-income Canadians save in RRSPs, the major beneficiary is the government," says Richard Shillington, an Ottawa-based tax policy analyst. "At retirement, many seniors who put money aside are made to pay for services that would otherwise be free, or they're forced to pay full price for services that would otherwise be subsidized."

Canada's income assistance for seniors starts with old age security (OAS), which is clawed back from individuals with incomes of $55,000 and over. Seniors who are less well off can get the guaranteed income supplement (GIS). Benefits are reduced by 50 cents for each dollar of RRSP income. For those who use home care and meals on wheels, or live in a nursing home or social housing, the costs of these services increase with income. The extra RRSP income can actually reduce a senior's standard of living.

A surprising number of low-income Canadians put money into RRSPs. In 1997, two million Canadians with incomes under $30,000 a year contributed $4 billion to RRSPs, according to Statistics Canada.

"Putting that much money away must have been quite a sacrifice," Shillington says, "but what many of them don't realize is, for all that sacrifice, they'll likely be rewarded with reduced government benefits at retirement."

You're in good shape contributing to an RRSP if you also have a company pension. Your pension will keep you off the guaranteed income supplement once you retire.

If you're married and both spouses work, your combined Canada Pension Plan payments will keep you off GIS. But if you're single with no pension or part of a single-income household, you shouldn't contribute to an RRSP—not unless you can sock away $200,000 or so by the time you retire.

"The worst thing is to have a $30,000 RRSP and take out $3,000 a year. You'll lose all your benefits," Shillington says. Don't worry. In his view you can qualify for income-tested social services and still have a comfortable retirement.

Here's Shillington's advice:

■ Buy a house. Most social programs don't take the value of your principal residence into account. Once you pay off the mortgage, a reverse mortgage allows you to "spend" the equity in your house without moving or affecting your eligibility for income-tested benefits (such as GIS).

- Invest outside an RRSP. When you cash in your investments at retirement, only the profit (and not the capital) affects your income-tested benefits. But when you withdraw money from an RRSP, the entire amount is added to your income.

- Use a spousal RRSP to split income. Suppose $60,000-a-year Tom contributes to a spousal plan for $20,000-a-year Mary. After three years, the money is hers. She can take it out at her lower tax rate and invest it outside the RRSP.

- Take money out of an RRSP before retirement. Pay the tax on it, then invest the money outside of an RRSP. Money withdrawn gradually from an RRSP is taxed and counted as income.

Don't count on early retirement

You set up a registered retirement savings plan and put away a little money each year. But you haven't a clue whether you're on the right track or not. Developing a financial plan for life after work means asking yourself two questions: When do I want to retire? And how well do I want to live in retirement? The answers will determine how much you need to save.

Let's start with age. According to life expectancy figures, the average 40-year-old man in Canada will live to almost 77, the average 40-year-old woman to 82. As people get older, their life expectancy improves. The average 65-year-old man can expect to live to 80, the average woman to 85.

Modern medicine is also leading to increased longevity. Those who are younger may have the delightful prospect of 30 more years of life to look forward to by the time they hit 65.

Most of us still consider 65 the normal retirement age, but it's not any more. A Statistics Canada survey found 71 per cent of retirees had stopped work before 65, and 34 per cent retired before 60. And more working Canadians start taking Canada Pension Plan benefits at age 60 to 64 than wait until 65.

This pattern of early retirement was caused by the downsizing wave that began in the early 1990s. Many people were forced out of full-time jobs by employer cutbacks before they were ready to go. The wave of early retirements also reflects higher levels of personal savings and a desire for "Freedom 55." London Life's slogan was the most successful marketing campaign ever launched by a Canadian financial services company. If only it were so easy!

Freedom 55 is an impossible dream for most people. You have to plan carefully and cut back severely on current consumption. In effect, you sacrifice everything that makes life wonderful today in favour of an unknown future.

If you haven't seriously begun to save for retirement by the time you're 40, you'll never accumulate enough capital to retire comfortably at 55 or 60. With fewer years to save money and more years to spend it, you run the risk of finding yourself in difficulty before you hit 70.

"I've seen it happen to people I know," says author Gordon Pape. "They quit their jobs in their 50s, believing they were in a reasonably good financial position. Within five years, they were back at work, sometimes full-time, earning enough to make ends meet."

Early retirees often start new careers, but run afoul of the "antique-shop syndrome." That's when you think it would be nice to run a business, but jump into something specialized without the necessary knowledge and skills. If you've always worked in a large organization, you may find it tough coping in a small business without the backup you're used to. It's not an easy adjustment.

"Instead, can you continue your current career on a part-time or seasonal basis? The workplace is becoming incredibly flexible," says author Bruce Cohen in *The Money Adviser* (Stoddart).

So the decision about retirement age involves more questions. When do you want to stop working full-time? Will you ease off gradually? Or will you start a new career? Your spouse's plans must be part of the picture.

Then you have to decide how well you want to live in retirement. "Comfortably," you say? That's not a good enough answer. You have to be more specific.

The younger you are, the harder it is to define your retirement goals. Still, you can compile a wish list.

Here are some questions each spouse should answer:

- Do you want to stay in your current house?

- If you sell your house, will you move to something less expensive or more expensive?

- Do you want to acquire a second residence?

- Do you want more time with family? Travel? Winters in the sun? Sports activities? Gardening? Hobbies? Part-time work? Volunteer or charitable work?

The next step is putting a price tag on your goals and estimating your expenses in retirement. You'll need to know approximately how much you spend now in each category. If you don't have a current budget, this is a good time to create one.

When it comes to housing, figure out whether you will discharge your mortgage by the time you stop work. Don't underestimate your home improvement expenses after retirement. You'll want to renovate and buy new furniture and appliances when you have more time on your hands.

If you want to buy a vacation property, estimate the purchase price. Then, assuming you need a mortgage, use 15 to 20 per cent of the estimated purchase price as the annual cost of carrying the property.

Some expenses typically go up in retirement and some go down. On the plus side, food costs less when your children leave home and you stop buying meals at work. Clothes may cost less if you no longer have to dress for work.

Life and disability insurance costs will come down, unless you want to use life insurance to leave a big estate to your children. Transportation may be cheaper if you and your spouse both have cars and you can get by with one. You may drive less without your daily commute, which means lower car insurance costs, too.

After retirement, you stop contributing to company pension plans and stop paying Canada Pension Plan and employment insurance premiums. And you can no longer make RRSP contributions once you and your spouse turn 69.

Family costs are hard to estimate. Your children will cost less as they complete their education and settle down. But as grandchildren come along, you may spend more for gifts and visits. And you may have to support elderly parents or other relatives.

Holidays and travel may well cost more once you quit work. Recreation costs, too, could soar if you're active and pursue lots of hobbies such as golf, gardening, boating, antique collecting and taking courses. "This is your chance to do all those things you complained you never had time for, so make sure the money is available in your budget," Pape says.

By the time you've put some numbers on your desired lifestyle, you may find it's more expensive to retire than you realized. That's all the more reason to keep working as long as you can.

Maybe you'll never retire

Want to reduce the risk of outliving your money? Don't retire. It's not as wacky as it sounds. Many people stay in the work force beyond age 60 or 65 if they're healthy and they enjoy what they're doing.

As you get older, you can tap into a whole world of income opportunities. You can work for your existing employer, full-time or part-time or on a seasonal basis. You can do freelance consulting, writing, teaching or counselling. You can find paid work in the charitable sector. Or you can run your own business.

Retirement is often expensive in the early years. You're fit and healthy and yearning to make up for all the things you missed while tied to a job. So you shell out big dollars for travel, recreation or even shopping. But when you're working, you have less time to spend money. And you're not touching your investments. Continuing to work lets you maintain your standard of living and not succumb to the ravages of inflation.

Work also offers psychological rewards: a feeling of purpose and identity, a social network, a chance to build new skills or use the ones you already have.

Randy Dutka is typical of many people who decide in mid-life to branch out into other areas. He's an actuary, someone who's good with numbers and helps control risk for companies that sell insurance policies and pension plans.

After his employer merged with another firm, Dutka decided to wind down his full-time career at age 54 and use his actuarial skills to start two freelance businesses. One business is dispute resolution, helping professional firms deal with squabbling partners. (He's seen the damage such fights can cause in his own career.)

His other business is teaching people how to gamble, based on his own time playing casino games and calculating the odds. "You can't make money gambling, but I tell people how to go to a casino and have a great time," he says. "I treat it as entertainment."

Before going into business for yourself, it's important to assess your strengths and weaknesses. Are you good at networking? Are you comfortable picking up the phone and making cold calls to strangers? Can you accept rejection without getting disheartened?

"When you're self-employed, you have to promote yourself and ask for business. Otherwise, you don't get it," Dutka advises.

Are you familiar with the Internet and email? Can you use tax and accounting programs? Clients demand technological proficiency as well as business experience.

It's smart to start planning your new business while you're still employed. And recognize you may need professional help for your company's name, logo, Web site, business cards, telephone system and banking and credit facilities.

A hazard for the newly self-employed is getting too much work too soon and not being able to cope. "You can't let clients down," Dutka warns. "Word gets out in a minute. It's not like you're the only person in the world."

Running your own business offers tax advantages, which can compensate for lower income in the early years. But you have to balance the hard work against your energy level. You may need to slow down as you get older.

A salaried job is easier to manage, especially if you can do similar work to what you do now (but part-time). You may find your employer is happy to cut a deal. With a demographic crunch resulting in fewer younger workers, companies will be more likely to agree to flexible arrangements that keep older workers on the job.

You may need professional help to decide what to do after retirement. The key is to replace the satisfactions lost from work.

Alan Roadburg, a Toronto retirement planner, interviewed 350 retirees aged 52 to 86 and discovered that 40 per cent were unhappy and bored. "Time and time again, I came across people who became disenchanted with retirement after the initial honeymoon phase ended," he says. "They got the travel bug out of their system, or they found that playing golf every day was not as much fun as they thought it would be."

A tenured university professor specializing in the sociology of aging, Roadburg switched gears to start a new career helping people find more challenges in retirement. For more than 15 years, he's given workshops to employees of General Motors, Unilever and the RCMP. He gets people working in groups to think up activities that will satisfy their souls.

Joe, for example, was a welder with a heavy equipment supplier. He planned to move to a small farm when he retired and open up a welding shop to earn extra money. But in a brainstorming session at a retirement workshop, Joe identified teaching as one of his skills that wouldn't be used, given his plans. So he came up with the idea of teaching welding when he moved.

Janet, another workshop participant, was planning to open a guest house when she retired. She loved animals but found that whenever she travelled, she had trouble finding a place for her pets. By putting this information together, she formed the idea of opening a guest house where people were encouraged to bring their pets—a service other guest houses didn't offer.

The word *retirement* carries a load of nasty imagery. To retire means to give up your work or business because of advancing age, to retreat or withdraw, to give ground, to pay off a debt, to go to sleep.

Roadburg uses a slightly different term, to "re-tire" (with the emphasis on the first syllable), which suggests getting a new set of wheels for a car. He says boomer re-tirees will be active, engaged and energetic. What they hope to gain from re-tirement is movement, action, rejuvenation, freedom and a fresh start.

Many employers offer lifestyle planning as a retirement benefit.

If you can't get it on the job, you can find courses in the community. Or contact the Canadian Association of Pre-Retirement Planners (CAPP), which has directory of members at: www.retirementplanners.ca.

Get to know your retirement benefits

When you leave the world of full-time work, you can count on three sources of income. You will be living on government benefits, company pensions and your own savings.

First there are the government benefits, Old Age Security (OAS) and Canada Pension Plan (CPP). Together, they're designed to replace up to 40 per cent of your pre-retirement income.

Old Age Security, which came into force in 1952, is the most comprehensive retirement program. If you're 65 or over and you've lived in Canada at least ten years, you're entitled to some OAS benefits (even if you have left the country). The maximum OAS pension is about $5,400 a year. It's fully indexed to inflation. You must apply for the money. It doesn't arrive automatically when you hit the right age.

Low-income retirees can also get the guaranteed income supplement (GIS). It provides a maximum of about $6,400 a year for a single person who has a retirement income of about $13,000.

But the OAS program is under attack by governments anxious to cut costs and you may not be able to count on it when you retire. The weapon of attack is the "clawback." In 1989, Finance Minister Michael Wilson decided that OAS recipients with more than $50,000 a year in net income had to pay back part of their benefits. The

$50,000 threshold was only partially indexed to inflation, meaning it drew in more retirees every year.

After protests by seniors' groups, Finance Minister Paul Martin restored full indexing to the tax system in 2000. This means the clawback threshold rises in line with inflation. The clawback threshold in the year 2002 is about $57,000. It's based on net income (total income minus tax deductions). If your net income is more than $57,000, you lose 15 cents of every $1 in benefits. The amount is deducted from your monthly payments. If you earn more than $93,000, you get no OAS benefits at all. The entire amount is taxed back before you receive it.

Since the clawback is based on individual income, not family income, you can minimize the impact through income splitting tactics. For example, you can make spousal RRSP contributions now to put money into the hands of a lower-income spouse.

"Pay off all debts before age 65 to reduce your income needs," say Bruce Cohen and Brian FitzGerald in *The Pension Puzzle* (John Wiley & Sons). "Similarly, make as many major purchases before age 65 as seems practical—for example, a new car."

Another way to reduce your income needs is to take Canada Pension Plan or Quebec Pension Plan before age 65 and share the benefits with your spouse. You can apply for a reduced CPP/QPP pension as early as 60. The Canada and Quebec Pension Plans, launched in 1966, cover only those in the paid work force. Full-time homemakers are not included, though they can share their spouse's retirement payments.

Most people now apply for CPP/QPP retirement benefits before they reach 65. Corporate downsizing accounts for part of this trend. There's also a popular perception that the plans are financially shaky and may not be around long enough for you to collect if you wait. Don't believe what you hear. The Canada and Quebec Pension Plans will be there when you retire. Governments have agreed to raise employee and employer contributions to a level that will sustain the plan indefinitely. The changes took effect in 1998.

CPP and QPP are not like employer pension plans, which must put aside money to pay promised benefits. They are funded primarily by contributions from active workers. It's "an intergenerational transfer," Cohen and FitzGerald explain: "In effect, money arrives in the morning and goes out in the afternoon."

There's a small surplus not needed to pay pensions, which is managed by an arm's length investment board. The idea is to build up the fund over time and use it to subsidize future contributions. You can keep tabs on how the CPP Investment Board is doing by reading the quarterly reports at its Web site, www.ccpib.ca.

At what age should you apply for CPP/QPP? Here are things to consider in deciding when to apply for retirement benefits:

- The size of your pension depends on how long you contributed to CPP and how much you contributed. The federal government sends out annual statements estimating how much you will get at 65. The maximum for 2002 is $9,600 a year.

- If you apply for CPP before 65, you must have stopped working. You can still earn a little, but no more than the pension you would have received at 65. Once you start getting CPP retirement benefits, you can work again if you want (either full-time or part-time). There's no clawback as with OAS.

- Your pension is reduced by 0.5 per cent a month for each month you receive the money before age 65. If you're 62, your pension is cut by 18 per cent. If you're 60, your pension is cut by 30 per cent.

- Even if you take a 30 per cent reduced pension at age 60, your five extra years' worth of payments will keep you ahead of someone who waited for a full pension at 65. The gap disappears only when you reach your mid-to-late 70s.

- If you want a bigger CPP benefit, you can put off collecting it beyond age 70. Your pension will go up 0.5 per cent a month for each month you wait. So, if you start at 70 (the top limit), your pension is 30 per cent higher.

- Your CPP payments are fully indexed to the cost of living and last as long as you do. They don't run out at a certain age.

By starting CPP early, you can avoid tapping your RRSP or registered retirement income fund for spending money. "You then prolong the tax-sheltered growth of these plans," say Cohen and FitzGerald.

If you contribute to the Canada Pension Plan (not the Quebec Pension Plan), you now get an annual statement showing your progress. This initiative is long overdue. While private pension plans must send statements to everyone once a year, the average CPP contributor used to get statements only every four or five years. The federal government was reluctant to mail out 13.5 million statements a year, but it had a remarkable change of heart. That's because it did a wide-ranging survey in 1999 that showed most people knew little about the CPP—and what they did know they didn't trust.

Knowledge of Old Age Security was only marginally better. "Canadians don't know how these plans work and that's why they don't understand the plans will be there for them," says a federal government official.

I tracked down the survey results and found them intriguing. "Can you name the Government of Canada public pension programs?" Almost half (41 per cent) could not name even one without assistance.

"Are all Canadians currently entitled to CPP when they retire?" More people gave the wrong answer than the right answer: 45 per cent said everyone is entitled to CPP, while only 38 per cent understood that you must contribute to get benefits.

"Provided the system remains as it is today, would you say that you have a good idea, some idea or no idea at all how much you personally might collect from CPP and OAS when you retire?" Good idea: 16 per cent. Some idea: 22 per cent. No idea: 60 per cent.

Despite the low literacy about public pensions, two out of three people said they didn't mind paying into CPP. They still value the idea of public pensions, even if they're sceptical about whether the programs can be sustained.

Annual pension statements are only the beginning. Government officials, with computers and printers, will go to public forums and produce personal pension statements while you wait. They're making the Web site for income security programs easier to navigate, adding calculators so you can work out your own figures.

The survey found people would not resent—and would actually welcome—more government information on pensions, as long as it was personal and detailed and not just propaganda. About 40 per cent rated Ottawa highly as a credible source on retirement planning, compared to 19 per cent who gave a high rating to companies that sell mutual funds.

Find out how your company pension works

After public pensions, your second source of retirement income is a company pension plan. About five million Canadians belong to one. Yet most members have no idea what kind of plans they have and how much will be provided when they retire.

Your employer should provide you with a personal pension statement every year, based on your current earnings. The closer you are to retirement, the more accurate the estimate will be. Put these statements into a folder with your Canada Pension Plan statements, which now arrive yearly as well.

Some pension statements look into the future to tell you how much you can expect to receive in retirement, assuming you stay in your job to age 60 or 65 and your eligible earnings remain the same. If you can't find an income projection, ask your plan administrator for one. That will tell you what percentage of your current income you can expect to receive as a pension.

I'm assuming you belong to a defined benefit pension plan. That's a safe bet, since most Canadian employees covered by pensions have a defined benefit plan. This is one in which the payment is determined by a fixed formula, based on your income and years of service. The amount you get is guaranteed.

It's harder to estimate what you will get with a defined contribution plan, which works like an RRSP. The pension you get relates to how much you and your employer contribute to the plan over the years and how well the investments perform. The end result is not guaranteed, but depends on stock market returns and interest rates. Still, it's worth asking your plan administrator to estimate the size of pension you will get from a defined contribution plan. You can suggest using current contribution rates and a conservative annual return, say 5 to 6 per cent.

The group RRSP is a newer type of plan, "spreading like wildfire since they let employers provide retirement plans at little or no administrative cost of effort," say Cohen and FitzGerald. With a group RRSP, the employer acts as administrator for a collection of individual RRSPs and deducts contributions from employees' pay. A member gets a choice of how the money is invested and an immediate tax saving on contributions, instead of having to wait until filing a tax return.

As soon as the money goes into a group RRSP, it's yours to withdraw whenever you like. (However, some employers put conditions on group RRSPs they subsidize.) It's much harder to withdraw money from a defined benefit or defined contribution plan. When you change jobs, the money is locked in until you reach a certain age (usually 50 to 55) or if you're facing financial hardship or shortened life expectancy.

Less than half of Canadian workers are covered by pension plans and the percentage has been declining in recent years. Consider yourself lucky if your employer has a plan, even if you think pensions are boring and only for security-conscious, middle-aged folks.

Here are questions to ask in order to understand your plan and get the most from it:

- What type of plan do I have? As well as defined benefit and defined contribution plans and group RRSPs, there are also deferred profit-sharing plans. Employers pay the full cost, using a share of company profits, and don't have to contribute if there was no profit for the year.

- What is the benefits formula? Some defined benefits plans base your pension on the salary you earned during your entire career with the company. Others base the payout on the average of your best three or five years' salary.

- Is my purchasing power protected? While indexed pension plans are common in the public sector, few private companies guarantee that payments will increase with the cost of living. Some plans are partially indexed and some companies make goodwill adjustments every few years. Find out about your company's track record.

- Will I keep my insurance benefits in retirement? Your pension will go further if you can hang on to benefits such as supplementary health and dental insurance, life insurance and coverage of pre-scription drugs. Companies are starting to cut back these benefits for retirees because of the high cost.

- When do I become vested? This is when you get the right to the pension benefits that were bought by your employer's contribu-tions. It's generally two to five years after you join the company or the pension plan.

While vesting gives you title to the employer's money, you gen-erally can't cash any pension credits until 10 years before the normal retirement age.

Here are your options if you leave your job after becoming vest-ed but before retirement:

- Leave the credits in the plan. Your old employer will manage the money and you will collect a pension based on your credits when you retire.

- Transfer the credits to a plan managed by your new employer, if that's allowed.

- Transfer the money to an insurance company to buy an annuity.

- Transfer the money to a locked-in registered retirement savings plan, also called a locked-in retirement account, which you will manage yourself.

The last option is the most popular. (I chose it when I changed jobs in 1997.) Locked-in RRSPs are just like regular RRSPs in terms of your investment choices. But there are special rules for withdrawals, which are designed to make the retirement income last a lifetime.

Each province has slightly different rules for locked-in retirement accounts. The questions you need to ask your human resources department or pension plan administrator are:

- Which province will regulate my locked-in plan?

- What's the earliest age I can withdraw the money?

- How much can I withdraw each year after retirement?

- Under what conditions can I get a lump-sum withdrawal before retirement?

Lump-sum withdrawals may be permitted if you're leaving Canada or you have a life-threatening disease. You may also be allowed to cash your locked-in RRSP if it's very small. Two provinces (Ontario and Quebec) allow withdrawals for those who fit narrowly defined conditions of financial hardship.

Early access to locked-in plans may not provide as much relief as you think. The withdrawal will be fully taxable as income and may affect your eligibility for social benefits. Also, the money you take out is no longer creditor-proof and may be seized by those to whom you owe money.

To sum up, your employer's pension plan may be great, middling or not so good. Find out what it is and how it works by reading the booklets you're given and talking to your human resources department or labour union. Bone up on your investment choices, if you have any to make.

The pension plan is something you look at when choosing a job. You don't have to make it a deal breaker. You can accept a challenging, well-paid job with a rotten pension plan (or no plan at all). But when you're offered similar jobs, you should gravitate to the one with the best pension plan and employee benefits.

With the right pension plan, you can retire at age 50 or 55 with an indexed pension for life—provided you stick around long enough. This is common in the public sector. "Police officers, nurses, teachers and many civil servants have good defined benefit pension plans, in part because they pay high contributions," say Bruce Cohen and Brian FitzGerald in *The Pension Puzzle* (John Wiley and Sons). "They also tend to have strong job security. And many public employee plans across Canada are so similar the members can transfer credits at full value."

However, many Canadians aren't as fortunate. They work in the private sector and change jobs often, so they don't qualify for the maximum benefits. Some work for companies that have no pension plans. Others are self-employed. These folks may have to top up the pensions they get from government and an employer with their own retirement savings plan. That's the role of the tax-sheltered RRSP.

Top up your pensions with an RRSP

What does it take to retire in comfort, outrun inflation and have enough money for a long healthy life? For most people, it requires either luck or discipline. You can't plan to win the lottery, inherit a fortune from a rich relative or make a windfall gain on your house. But you can plan to set aside a certain number of dollars each year. That's something within your control.

If you save systematically, you'll get more bang for your buck by using a registered retirement savings plan. Since 1957, the government has given Canadians a tax break by letting them deduct RRSP contributions against their other income.

Depending on your income and marginal tax rate, you will get back 30 to 40 per cent or more of what you put into an RRSP. The tax refund is so attractive that some people make a contribution for that reason alone.

The government also lets you postpone paying tax on the money your RRSP earns until you take it out of the plan. That's another tax break and it's more valuable the longer your money stays in the plan (because of the tax-free compounding).

I like the RRSP for another reason. By using this tax shelter, your money is sheltered from temptation. Once your cash is inside, you have to jump through hoops to get it back. There are forms to fill out and taxes to pay—at least 10 per cent deducted off the top and more to pay at tax filing time.

With limited access to your money, you can be a more disciplined saver. You're less likely to liquidate the fund to pay for vacations and other indulgences. The desire to spend may disappear while you're waiting up to a week for withdrawals.

I also like the flexibility. An RRSP can be used to finance a down payment on a first house or to pay for your own or your spouse's higher education. You can use it as an emergency fund to draw down during periods of unemployment or parental leave.

There's no penalty to take money from an RRSP before retirement. You do have to repay the tax you saved earlier. But if you're in a lower tax bracket than when you contributed, you'll end up ahead. This is why the RRSP works as an income stabilizer when you're out of work or staying home with the kids.

What's the key to success? Make contributions all year round, not just during the annual RRSP advertising blitz. Ask your financial institution to debit your account by a fixed amount on a regular basis, say once a month, and put it into your RRSP right away.

Some people think an RRSP is an investment. "I bought an RRSP," they say. If you ask what's inside, they don't know. "It's an RRSP," they say again, showing you their receipt.

Try to think of an RRSP as a filing cabinet, a secure receptacle where you store different kinds of investments. You may have your savings account in the top drawer, guaranteed investment certificates in the second drawer, mutual funds in the third drawer, company shares in the bottom drawer. Just as a filing cabinet keeps your papers safe from intruders, an RRSP keeps your investments safe from the tax man. You pay tax on the earnings only when you pull an investment out of a drawer.

Putting money into an RRSP is just the first step. Then you have to pick the investments and watch them to make sure they're doing well. You can't take your eyes off the plan for very long.

A filing cabinet, too, requires monitoring. What good is it if you don't have the right documents in the right place?

Sometimes people get sloppy because of the last-minute rush. The government gives everyone two extra months, January and February, to make an RRSP contribution for the previous year. So it's natural to wait for the deadline before you act.

Here's a typical late-February transaction. You go into the bank and talk to someone who gives you a number of investment choices. You don't know what to do, but you know it's important to get your money into an RRSP before it's too late. You want that tax refund.

So you put $3,000 into an RRSP savings account and you leave. You're earning almost nothing (0.75 per cent), but that's OK. You'll make time to figure out your investments later, when it's not so busy. Months go by and you do nothing. There are more important things on your mind. Soon it's February again and your RRSP statement arrives in the mail. You're embarrassed to see you've earned a grand total of $67.50 on your savings. If you had put the money in a guaranteed investment certificate paying two per cent, you could have made $180 (more than twice as much). That's the cost of inattention.

So don't think only about the tax refund. While gratifying, it's not the only benefit of an RRSP. The tax-free compound growth is a bigger bonus if you keep your savings in the plan for many years.

But you won't have much growth if you're content to let your money sit in a low-interest savings account. This should be only a temporary parking place.

The solution: Keep track of your RRSP investments. Ask your financial institution to send you statements more than once a year. Sign up for online access, so you can check your progress any time.

And remember that an RRSP is not an investment. It's a legal arrangement that lets you defer tax on your earnings for many years. But it won't do the job for you unless you have real earnings.

For the nitty-gritty on RRSPs, you can get a helpful free guide from the Canada Customs and Revenue Agency. Look for T4040, "RRSPs and Other Registered Plans for Retirement," at the CCRA's Web site, www.ccra-adrc.gc.ca, or call 1-800-959-2221.

Here's a brief summary of the rules:

- You must have earned income to contribute to an RRSP. There's no minimum age. Even children can set up an RRSP with money earned from babysitting or another part-time job.

- To know how much you can contribute to an RRSP, check the notice of assessment you received after your last tax return was processed. It usually comes in May or June if you file before the April 30 tax deadline.

- You can contribute up to 18 per cent of your earned income, or a maximum of $13,500, in a year. If your assessment notice shows a higher limit, it's because you didn't contribute the maximum in previous years. You can carry forward RRSP room you did not use.

- If your RRSP limit is lower than 18 per cent of your earned income or $13,500, it's because you have a company pension plan or deferred profit-sharing plan. Members of top-quality pension plans get little or no RRSP room at all.

- You can contribute to an RRSP in one year and claim the deduction in a future year. This is a good thing to do if you expect to be in a higher tax bracket later and you want a bigger tax refund.

- Parents can put $2,000 into an RRSP for a child who's at least 18, even if he or she has no RRSP-eligible income. (Anyone over 18 has a $2,000 over-contribution limit.) The child gets an early start on saving and can deduct the $2,000 against his or her income at a later date.

- You can use some or all of your RRSP contribution room for a spouse or common-law partner. Your goal is not to save taxes today, but to equalize the two spouses' incomes in retirement and pay less in taxes.

Spousal RRSPs work well in families like mine. I work at a big company that has a good pension plan, while my husband is self-employed and has no pension and little money put aside.

I expect to have a higher retirement income, so I'll pay a higher tax rate on my RRSP withdrawals. My husband's tax rate will be much lower. By putting money into his hands now through a spousal RRSP, I keep more of my hard-earned savings later. We will save tax as a family and reduce the impact of the Old Age Security clawback.

A cautionary note about spousal plans: The money becomes your partner's property right away. However, if your spouse makes a withdrawal in the first few years, the money will be taxed at your higher rate.

Is it worth borrowing to buy an RRSP? Yes, if you can pay back the loan within a year. Use your tax refund to discharge the debt more quickly. The interest on an RRSP loan is not tax-deductible, the way interest on other investment loans is.

But think twice about RRSP loans that let you catch up on contributions you were entitled to, but did not use, in several previous years. "Consider that if you really lack discipline," say Bruce Cohen and Brian FitzGerald in *The Pension Puzzle* (John Wiley & Sons). "Otherwise, you might do better by simply starting a monthly investment plan with contributions that equal what the loan payment would have been.

"Ask your financial adviser or banker to project both scenarios over 10 years and 20 years and compare the results."

It's never too late to start an RRSP

Diane, a *Toronto Star* reader, called me a few months before her fiftieth birthday. "Do you have any advice for late starters?" she asked.

Diane owned a successful cookware store in Toronto. While excellent at business, she hadn't paid much attention to her personal finances. She had little set aside for the time she stopped working. And, like most baby boomers, she hoped never to retire.

Her dilemma is fairly common, says Gordon Pape in *Retiring Wealthy in the 21st Century*. "Despite repeated urging, many people just can't get serious about retirement planning until the target date for stopping work starts to show up on their personal radar scopes."

Diane realized it was time to think about a retirement plan. What she really wanted to know: Am I too late? Have I missed the boat?

To sort out her money questions, I enlisted the help of Warren Baldwin, a fee-only financial planner at TE Financial Consultants Ltd. He studied her personal finances for several months. Barbara can stop working at 65 and live comfortably, he said. As her income from the store grows, she can start making contributions to an RRSP. But Baldwin wanted her to skip the RRSP contribution for the current year. She had more pressing financial needs, such as getting disability insurance and paying off some expensive dental bills.

Here was Diane's financial situation:

- She took income of $30,000 a year from her store, spent all she earned, but had no debt.

- Though she had split up with her husband four years earlier and lived apart from him, she was not legally separated. They shared custody of a 14-year-old daughter. Things were amicable, both socially and financially, she said.

- Her husband lived in the family home, worth $400,000 but still mortgaged. She rented an $875-a-month apartment nearby, a short walk from the store.

- Neither spouse had a pension plan. Neither would receive an inheritance. Together, they had RRSPs worth $90,000.

- She had $20,000 in guaranteed investment certificates, which had been used as collateral for a credit line to buy $70,000 worth of store inventory. She no longer needed that credit.

Warren Baldwin recommended that Diane formalize the separation with her husband. This would allow each of them to make some long-term financial plans.

Her husband, who earned $75,000 a year as a sales manager, could boost his cash flow by selling the house and renting near his daughter's school. After selling the house, he could catch up on missed RRSP contributions (some of which could be spousal plans in his wife's name, if he agreed to do so).

Diane could use her GICs to pay out her husband's debt on the house, then ask him to lend her $20,000 to resecure the line of credit. Though the credit line was not currently used, it was important to keep for future business needs.

As a small-business owner, Diane needed disability insurance. "While this is expensive—about $100 a month—not having it is a serious hole in her finances," Baldwin said. "If she's disabled, she may not lose the store, but she'd have no income and be unable to continue."

He felt she could wait a year to make an RRSP contribution, when her income was higher and the tax refund worth more. Or she could contribute in the current year, but not claim the deduction till the following year.

Baldwin made five assumptions about Diane's retirement plan:

- She would begin making $36,000 in annual income from the store and contribute $6,000 a year ($500 a month) to an RRSP between age 50 and age 65.

- Half of the couple's RRSPs (or $45,000) belonged to her.

- Her living expenses in retirement would be 70 per cent of her current spending.

- Inflation would run at three per cent a year.

- Her RRSP investments would be very simple (82 per cent in a no-load, low-cost balanced fund and 18 per cent in an international equity fund).

He also advised Diane and her husband to find out how much they would qualify to receive in Canada Pension Plan benefits when they retired. To help her look ahead, he calculated two CPP scenarios.

If she received the maximum CPP benefit of $9,000 a year (indexed), she would have a comfortable retirement. Her estate would be worth about $300,000 at age 90.

But Diane wouldn't get the maximum benefit, since she'd taken seven years off to return to school and raise her child. She'd probably earn about $5,000 a year in CPP, which meant she would use up most of her capital and RRSP savings in retirement. Her total estate at age 90 would be $65,000.

Diane's reaction: "I learned how little CPP provides. That was a shock."

While she was getting quotes on a disability policy ("it costs more like $200 a month, not $100 as Warren said") and checking out ethical funds for her RRSP, she was dragging her feet on a request to fill out forms outlining her budget.

"I know it's valuable to track my expenses," she said. "But I'm here in the store 10 to 14 hours a day, six days a week. This requires more time than I'm capable of."

Diane was relieved to hear she could save enough to stop working at age 65, despite her late start. But she planned to keep going anyway.

"I've had a new career every five to 10 years," she told me. "This store is a fulfilment of one of my dreams, but life is so short and there are so many things to do. I don't foresee ever not working."

Build a nest egg outside an RRSP

If you're serious about saving for retirement, an RRSP may not be enough for you. Some people have limited RRSP contribution room and more money to invest, perhaps from an inheritance or a year-end bonus. The key questions are: When do I start? And how do I balance this against my other financial priorities?

You can start a saving plan with your first RRSP contribution. Simply invest the tax refund you get after filing your tax return. Buying a labour-sponsored fund for your RRSP will generate additional tax credits, which can be invested outside the plan. Think twice about doing this, however, if you have outstanding credit card balances, loans or mortgages. Your money will be put to better use paying off your debt.

Don't worry if you don't have the disposable income to finance both a registered and non-registered retirement portfolio. Building non-RRSP assets can take a back seat to other needs. The time for most people to set up a portfolio outside an RRSP is in their mid-40s, says Gordon Pape in *Retiring Wealthy In The 21st Century* (Pearson Education Canada).

Since you will pay tax on the income from your non-RRSP portfolio, your money won't grow as quickly as in a tax-sheltered environment. Other financial priorities come first.

Once you get to the stage of life where you have extra cash and no loans to pay off, you should consider keeping some of your assets outside of an RRSP. You never know what the government will do in the future. Political or tax changes may affect your investments 25 years from now, a risk most Canadians overlook.

"Is it a safe, sound retirement planning approach to have almost all of your voluntary savings in any single investment strategy?" asks Talbot Stevens, an author and educator based in London, Ontario.

Financial advisers often encourage people saving for retirement to borrow money to invest. This strategy, known as "leveraging," magnifies returns, so it can be very profitable when used properly. But it can also cause you to lose more money than you otherwise would have.

Stevens compares leveraging to a power tool. Depending on how it used, it can either help you or harm you. "If we use a power saw carefully and responsibly, we might be able to saw ten times as quickly as we could with a hand saw," he says in his self-published booklet, *Dispelling the Myths of Borrowing to Invest*. "If we use the same hand saw carelessly without the appropriate precautions and guards in place, we could get hurt."

Stevens sells a $49.99 software program, Leverage Professional, to help people calculate how they could benefit from conservative borrowing. There's a free 30-day trial version at his Web site, www.talbotstevens.com.

I'm not a big fan of leveraging. I've seen too many people get hurt. Financial advisers often persuade older clients to borrow against their home to buy mutual funds. Here's how the sales pitch goes.

If you pay off your mortgage, are you really much further ahead? Your home equity does nothing for you. Why not use that equity as collateral for an investment loan? When you borrow to invest, you can deduct the full cost of your interest expenses each year. This produces the same tax savings as an RRSP contribution.

There's another tax break, too. Your equity mutual funds will grow tax-free, just as in an RRSP. You only pay tax when you sell, but remember that capital gains are only partially taxed. (You'll pay tax on your dividends or annual distributions, but that's no big deal.)

In fact, why bother with an RRSP at all when leveraging can produce the same tax breaks? Instead of an RRSP limit of up to $13,500 a year, you can borrow $50,000 or $100,000 and get a head start on your retirement savings. If the market's going up, you'll make more money.

Also, the government says you have to keep 70 per cent of your RRSP investments in Canada. This means you'll have lower returns than if you invest outside Canada. The domestic market is tiny (just 2 per cent of the world's equity) and doesn't offer as many opportunities. With a leveraging program, there are no foreign content rules. You can invest internationally as much as you like, without letting Ottawa tell you what to do.

Later in life, you get to keep more of your money if it's outside an RRSP. You will pay tax on just half of your capital gains. And you'll be able to use your capital losses to offset your gains. With an RRSP, withdrawals are taxed at the highest rate. You lose the tax break on capital gains and losses. And you're treated as if you had put all your money into heavily taxed interest investments.

This sales pitch works. That's why financial advisers love to use it at seminars. People come in thinking they have no extra money to invest and then realize they have equity lying dormant in their homes.

But you have to remember that commission-paid mutual fund dealers have a conflict of interest. Their livelihood depends on how much you invest with them. Clients who borrow $50,000 or $100,000 at a time are more lucrative than those who put smaller amounts in an RRSP.

Beware of a financial adviser who inflates the benefits and minimizes the risks of borrowing to invest. If you go into a leveraging program, make sure you're told exactly how much money you can lose if stock markets tank. Ask your adviser to crunch the numbers to generate a worst-case scenario.

Many people borrow to invest because they see only the upside. They're fair weather investors, unprepared to wait five to ten years to see how the strategy works. Market declines make them panic. They hate watching their investments shrink in value while they continue to pay interest on their loans.

Meanwhile, their financial advisers may be missing in action. They got them into this predicament and now they're not around to urge patience. Instead, they've moved on to new clients.

Leveraged investors may not last through a protracted downturn. They grow more anxious the longer their equity funds languish. Eventually, they can't take it any more. They pull the trigger and sell everything at a loss. The result: They still owe money on their investment loans. If they can't pay the balance, they end up with more debt. They're bitter and turned off investing forever. And who can blame them? That's why I think leveraging is dangerous for all but the most sophisticated and experienced investors. Everyone else should pay cash.

It's hard enough to sit tight while your investments go down. Why make it worse by burdening yourself with interest payments (even if they are tax-deductible)? This is a formula for failure.

One day, you will get to a stage of life when you can afford to start a second retirement savings plan. From a tax point of view, it makes sense to keep all interest investments inside your RRSP and all stocks and equity funds outside your RRSP. By segregating your investments that way, you will pay less tax. And as a bonus, you will be taking less risk with your RRSP funds.

Since you're limited in how much you can contribute to an RRSP, you should try to keep the money as safe as possible. Once lost, it can't be replaced.

When you hold equities outside an RRSP, you get tax breaks for your capital gains and losses. And, of course, you can add more money to replace what you might have lost.

Your home is not your retirement plan

Suppose you never get around to saving for retirement. Instead, you use every bit of extra cash to pay off your mortgage. Finally, you own your home free and clear. Is it enough to retire debt-free? The answer depends on whether or not you plan to stay in your house.

Though you've paid off the mortgage, you'll have other expenses. There will be property taxes to pay, electricity and gas bills, home insurance premiums, routine maintenance costs. As you get older, you may have to employ others to do jobs you once did yourself, such as snow removal, gardening and heavy cleaning.

Many retired people are house-rich and cash-poor. Their wealth is locked up in their property, but they can't get it out. Meanwhile, they're struggling to pay the ever-increasing costs of home ownership.

No longer employed, they may not qualify for conventional loans or secured lines of credit. The only financing they can get is from a mortgage broker at a higher cost. But they're reluctant to take on debt again after working so long to get rid of it.

If you're house-rich and cash-poor, what are your options? Well, you can stay in your home and rent out space to tenants. This assumes you have extra rooms and can provide some privacy. Also, you don't mind dealing with tenants and the repairs they always ask you to do.

You have to check your local bylaws, which may prohibit renting to tenants. Be aware, too, that you will have to pay capital gains tax on the part of your house used for rental when you sell. Normally, the gain on a principal residence is tax-free.

Another option is to sell the house, buy something smaller, invest the difference and live on the income. But there has to be a big price difference between the two properties to make it worthwhile, after paying moving and closing costs. You will have to downsize a lot or move to a less desirable location.

Also, there's a problem if your investments generate too much income. You could lose some income-tested benefits and have your old age pension taxed away. Paradoxically, you may have to put your money into a low-interest savings account to avoid clawbacks.

You can also sell the house, invest the proceeds and rent instead. But renting is expensive, especially if you live a long time after you retire. As you become less capable of caring for yourself, you will have to hire help at home or move into a long-term care facility. This will add to your costs.

No matter what you do with your house, you probably won't have enough to finance a long and comfortable life after retirement. You will also need a steady stream of income, which you can only get from pensions or investments.

"Ironically, while the home is a powerful symbol of independence and freedom, this valuable asset can also become a bittersweet financial burden for some home owners," says retirement housing expert PJ Wade in her book, *Have Your Home And Money Too* (John Wiley & Sons). You can read excerpts at her Web site, www.thecatalyst.com

Another option is to get a reverse mortgage. This allows retirees to convert their home equity into cash without selling the home. They don't repay any of the loan (principal or interest) while they live in the house. Everything is paid off from their estate when they die or sell the property.

The Canadian Home Income Plan (CHIP), founded in 1986, advertises that eligible seniors age 62 and older can get $20,000 to $500,000 from their homes. Since it's a loan, the income is not taxable and doesn't reduce the Old Age Security pension.

"We guarantee that your home is never at risk," CHIP promises in its newspaper ads and at its Web site, www.chip.ca. The plan is sold through several major banks, including the Royal Bank of Canada, the Toronto Dominion Bank and the Bank of Nova Scotia. Gordon Pape acts as the spokesman in CHIP's television commercials and longer infomercials.

Credit unions in Ontario also provide reverse mortgage lines of credit, Wade says. Unlike CHIP's product, such a line of credit is not restricted to those 62 or older, and you can repay it as you go.

Say you own a home worth $150,000. A reverse mortgage will give you $45,000 to $60,000, at most, since lenders cover a maximum of 30 to 40 per cent of the equity. There are appraisal and legal costs as well.

The older you are, the more the reverse mortgage will provide. And if you take the money in the form of an annuity (a fixed monthly income for life), your annuity payments will be higher if you're older, because you have less time to live and draw the payments.

But there are drawbacks. "People have no idea of how quickly the reverse mortgage accumulates through compounding," says Wade. "In 20 years, you may find the money is gone and the reverse mortgage has eaten up the entire property value. You can't afford to move and you can't afford not to move."

Anyone considering a reverse mortgage should get independent legal advice from someone who has experience with this complicated financial transaction and does not work for the lender. Unless a reverse mortgage fits you exactly, it's an expensive solution.

If you would be as happy in another house or condo, then selling and moving is your best strategy. A reverse mortgage may be the answer if no other house will suit you and you're sure you want to stay there for the rest of your life.

Putting a reverse mortgage on your home means your adult children will lose part of their inheritance. They need to be consulted about your plans.

"If you're in financial need, your children may prefer making regular payments to you themselves, in exchange for keeping the house unencumbered so it can pass to them at some time in the future," Gordon Pape says in *The Canadian Mortgage Guide* (Prentice Hall Canada).

You have started saving for retirement and you think you're on the right track, given your age and goals. But how do you know?

You can start by picking up free retirement planning booklets from your financial institution. There are also many good Web sites, with retirement calculators that show how much your savings will grow by the time you're ready to retire and how much income you will need to supplement your pensions.

But why settle for a one-size-fits-all solution? Isn't it better to get a retirement plan that's personalized and custom-made for you? That's the job of a financial adviser. I'm a firm believer in getting outside help, but I understand the natural reluctance to do it. There are too many horror stories about unscrupulous advisers putting their own interests ahead of those of their clients.

Here's a job posting for the ideal candidate:

- My financial adviser knows I'm different from everyone else in the world and will take the time to study my unique needs.

- My financial adviser listens to what I say. I want someone who gives me the freedom to say what's on my mind.

- My financial adviser doesn't overpower me. If I tape record our conversations, I find I'm talking at least half the time.

- My financial adviser is sensitive to my communication needs. Right from the start, we set up a schedule of face-to-face meetings and telephone calls. I dictate how often we will talk.

- My financial adviser gets in touch right away when there's a crisis in the markets or the economy.

- My financial adviser sends written statements I can understand and is willing to review them with me.

- My financial adviser tells me how well I'm doing and gives me a percentage rate of return on my entire portfolio.

- My financial adviser compares my progress against relevant and appropriate benchmarks.

A financial planning professional will use realistic assumptions about inflation and investment returns, says Catherine Hurlburt, a former president of the Canadian Association of Financial Planners. That's the value he or she brings to the table.

For example, a homemade retirement plan may use a three per cent inflation rate and a 10 per cent investment return. That's not realistic. There should be a gap of four percentage points, at most, between inflation and investment returns.

When looking for a financial planner, start by asking your friends and relatives for referrals. Make sure they're in the same financial position as you are, more or less. You don't want someone who's right out of your league.

There are two organizations that represent financial planners in Canada. They have announced plans to merge, which is welcome news. But until this happens, you can contact either or both and get help finding someone who works in your area.

The Canadian Association of Financial Planners has 2,700 practitioners with professional designations. They all carry liability insurance, obey a code of ethics and upgrade their education each year. Call 1-800-346-2237, or (416) 593-6592 in Toronto. The Web site is www.cafp.org.

The Financial Planners Standards Council is a larger group, with 14,000 members in Canada licensed to hold the internationally recognized professional designation Certified Financial Planner (CFP). Call 1-800-305-9886, or (416) 593-8587, in Toronto. The Web site is www.cfp-ca.org.

Governments have been slow to set standards for this fast-growing profession. The title of financial planner is not yet regulated, except in Quebec. So you have to be vigilant when looking for advice.

Here are 10 questions to ask a financial adviser:

- What is your educational background and training? Tell me, in writing if possible, exactly what courses you have taken and what professional designations you have earned.

- How long have you been in practice? What are your specialties?

- How are you paid? Do you charge fees, commissions or a combination of both? (In Canada, commission-based planners far outnumber fee-based planners.)

- Do you have a registration or disclosure document that gives your method of compensation, business affiliations and possible conflicts of interest?

- Can you give me references from clients?

- Do you work with other professionals, such as accountants, insurance brokers and lawyers? Can you give me references from them?

- Do you have assistants who handle client communications? Under what circumstances will I speak to them or to you? Can I get their names and meet them?

- Will you give me a written letter of engagement that outlines the services you will provide?

- Have you ever been disciplined by a regulatory body or industry organization? (Double-check the answer by contacting the relevant group.)

- Do you subscribe to a professional code of ethics? Have you taken a course in ethics?

The Investment Funds Institute of Canada, for example, offers an optional course for financial advisers in how to act ethically. The course material relies heavily on actual cases of wrongdoing, lawsuits and disciplinary action.

In one case study, an adviser named Sandy persuaded a client named Fred to sell a government bond fund and replace it with a more speculative growth fund. When Fred had opened the account a few years earlier, he told Sandy he wanted regular income. That was at a time when interest rates were higher. Sandy hadn't updated Fred's records since then.

Was it ethical for Sandy to cash in the bond fund, even if he sincerely believed returns would be higher with a stock fund? No, it wasn't. Buying speculative stocks was contrary to Fred's stated objectives when he opened the account. Sandy should have asked if Fred's objectives had changed and updated the file.

In another example, an adviser, Sheila, recommended that a semi-retired couple put a mortgage on their house to buy growth funds. She said they could pay the mortgage interest by selling fixed-income investments they held in their registered retirement savings plan. The RRSP withdrawals would be tax-free because they could deduct mortgage interest on their taxes.

Was it ethical to give such advice to unsophisticated investors? No, it wasn't. Sheila's recommendation was inappropriate, since she told the couple "to eliminate a predictable investment designed to finance retirement and enter a high-risk leverage program that has unpredictable results," the ethics course said.

A third case study involved Paula, who set up her own mutual fund dealership and borrowed $50,000 from several fund management companies. She promised to repay the loans out of future commissions she earned on selling the funds.

Was this ethical? No, it wasn't. Paula had a conflict of interest since she'd have to recommend certain funds to repay the loans, whether the funds suited her clients or not. She should disclose the conflict and give people the choice of buying her recommended funds or not.

Do you want to pay for advice?

If you're concerned about conflicts of interest, you should consult a fee-for-service financial planner. This is someone who is paid only for advice and doesn't sell any financial products.

It can be hard for those who live in smaller centres to find fee-for-service planners. They represent only five to 10 per cent of all financial advisers in Canada.

Most financial advisers make their living by selling stocks, bonds, guaranteed investment certificates, mutual funds, insurance or annuities. They don't charge for advice. The commissions they get from product suppliers pay for the time they spend with you.

The public seems to like it that way. In a 1999 survey by the Financial Planners Standards Council of Canada, only 16 per cent of the respondents said they wanted an adviser only to develop a plan. Most said they preferred financial planning and implementation bundled together.

Still, you're more likely to get objective advice if you go to someone who doesn't sell any products. I often refer people to fee-only financial advisers when I'm asked for referrals. I do this when people are at a turning point in their lives (retirement, inheritance, divorce or death of a spouse) and they need broad overall direction.

It's true that fee-only advisers don't implement a plan. Nevertheless, they can recommend a network of professionals to go to if you need help. You're not left completely stranded.

You can find out how a financial planner is compensated by asking questions. Or you can consult the two national associations of financial planners. They list such information in their printed and online directories.

As a fallback plan, you can look for a commission-paid adviser who also works for a fee. Many do. Find someone who's happy to prepare a financial or retirement plan for you without putting it into action. The cost will range from $500 to $3,000 or more, depending on the adviser's hourly rate.

Investment counsellors and discretionary money managers also charge fees. These are people who invest your money without consulting you on every transaction. They charge a flat annual fee based on a percentage of your assets under management.

You need substantial assets to hire an investment counsellor. The minimum portfolio size is generally $500,000, but many firms won't accept clients with under $1 million in assets. The average fee for a $500,000 portfolio is 1.5 per cent of assets, or $7,500 a year.

Investment counsellors get paid whether they trade or not. They have no incentive to "churn" a client's account by doing excessive or unnecessary trading. Churning is a risk with commission-paid advisers.

Robert's experience serves as a warning. A 40-year-old *Toronto Star* reader, he asked my advice about his locked-in retirement account. The portfolio had lost about a quarter of its value in the 15 months from February 2000 to May 2001. A loss of that size is not unusual in a bear market. But the hectic trading in his account was certainly out of the ordinary.

Robert had moved his account to a bank-owned investment dealer after getting a referral from his mother's bank. At the time, he had eight equity funds and four money market funds, worth $90,000. He told his financial adviser, in writing, to buy only mutual funds and not stocks.

The adviser ignored his instructions. He bought 20 stocks and sold 12 of them in little over a year. "Too many for my expectations," says Robert, who calculates the adviser earned $3,980 in commissions for the stock transactions. In some cases, the stocks were held for just one week before being sold.

The investment dealer reviewed the case and concluded the adviser had acted fairly. It gave three reasons:

- When Robert opened the account, he signed a client profile saying his objectives were 50 per cent growth and 50 per cent aggressive trading. He said he could handle 50 per cent medium- and 50 per cent high-risk investments.

- Robert authorized all the trades in his account. He could have rejected his adviser's recommendations.

- The investment dealer sent Robert confirmations of each purchase and sale, as well as monthly statements.

Robert should have raised his concerns immediately, said the firm's compliance officer. "The inaction on your part may be construed as deemed acceptance of the status of your account."

While admitting he didn't pay enough attention, Robert says he was unemployed and looking for work when he moved his account. When the adviser filled out a client profile for him to sign, he didn't realize how significant the document was. He had given specific instructions and thought he and his adviser were on the same wavelength.

Churning can be measured in different ways. One is the portfolio turnover rate, the total cost of your purchases divided by your average net equity for one year.

A turnover rate of two gives no excessive cause for concern, says Neil Gross, a Toronto lawyer who often represents investors in lawsuits against brokers. A turnover rate of four is suspicious. A turnover rate of six is very serious and should set off alarm bells.

Another test is the rate of return the portfolio would have had to achieve to overcome the cost of trading. Suppose a conservative portfolio could be expected to earn a return of 10 per cent in a given time period, but needed a 20 per cent return to cover commissions, interest and fees. If so, there's cause for concern that the portfolio is being churned, Gross says.

The moral: Watch your financial adviser really carefully. Check every document you sign and every statement that comes in the mail. Commission-paid advisers have an incentive to get you trading more actively and buying more risky stocks. If that's not your style, speak up right away. Talk to your adviser as soon as you see a pattern of churning. Don't wait or you may be too late.

Beware of free investment seminars

"Free seminar," scream the newspaper ads that sprout like mushrooms from December to February. Fronted by a prominent author or media personality, the seminars promise to teach you everything you need to know but never learned about getting rich.

In just an hour, you'll find out how to cut taxes, create wealth in turbulent markets, retire comfortably, invest without using your RRSP foreign content, leave more money to your heirs, move your savings offshore and live better and smarter.

By all means, go and listen and learn—but be extra careful when it comes to giving out personal details and allowing the sponsor to review your investments. You're offering yourself up as a valuable prospect to a stockbroker, mutual fund dealer, life insurance agent, banker or other financial intermediary hungry for new clients.

Don't put your trust in wisdom dispensed by financial gurus at gatherings of several hundred people. The person giving the advice with such authority may not even be licensed as a financial adviser. And there's no such thing as one-size-fits-all rules. Your financial situation is as individual as you are.

Consumer advocate Glorianne Stromberg says seminar speakers should disclose up front who's paying them and what sort of compensation they receive. As well as fees of $5,000 to $10,000, speakers may also earn a share of the sponsor's profits if enough audience members turn into clients.

Sometimes speakers give examples of investments they like, without disclosing they have a financial interest in these investments. "Too often, consumer/investors are influenced by the speaker's comments and end up losing a lot of money," Stromberg said in a report on mutual funds and consumer protection, sponsored by the federal government.

There's a kind of "halo effect" that allows sponsors to cash in on the appeal of popular media commentators such as Jerry White, Garth Turner and Brian Costello. These financial personalities dispense bland, generic advice, laced with humour and anecdotes.

The Ontario Securities Commission took action against Costello in early 2002, saying he was giving financial advice without a license and recommending investments in which he had an indirect financial interest. The charges have not yet been decided.

There's only one reason the sponsors fork out the high speaker's fees: They want to attract new prospects. That means you. Seminars are a popular way for financial advisers to draw new clients into their fold. How do they get your business? Usually painlessly, by asking you to participate in a draw for a free prize.

I know this first-hand, because I spent a lot of time on the seminar circuit a few years ago. (I don't do it any more.) One winter, I worked at my newspaper job all day and then drove an hour or more to speak at seminars in Barrie, Orangeville or Burlington. I did this three evenings a week for six weeks.

I got to choose lucky tickets out of a bowl or bin. The winners got prizes ranging from books to organizers to free mutual fund contributions. Sometimes a sponsor forgot to line up a prize and rushed out to find a store that stocked a few copies of *The Wealthy Barber*, a popular personal finance guide.

It was unthinkable not to have a raffle of some kind. Awarding prizes provided entertainment value, that's for sure. But even more important, it gave the financial adviser a list of people who had attended the seminar. You qualified for a prize by filling in your name, address and phone number. Often, you had to tick off yes or no to a question like this: "Do you want a free consultation on your investment portfolio?"

For the sponsor, a seminar's success was measured by how many people agreed to come in for an appointment. The numbers were watched very carefully. I remember one sponsor who always invited me for a post-seminar drink. As we talked, his assistant counted the number of Yes replies to see if the evening was a boon or a bust.

This sponsor—let's call him Joe—also urged me to say in my speeches, "When you go to see Joe for your free appointment." Not "if you go," but "when."

In the years since, I've attended a few financial seminars as an observer and seen the same routine still used. Not every sponsor asks if you're willing to have a meeting before giving you a follow-up call. Some try to recruit everyone who comes to the seminar and writes down his or her name for a prize draw. There's nothing wrong with this way of doing business, as long as the audience knows what to expect. First-time attendees rarely do.

I'm also concerned about the kind of advice dispensed at these seminars. Here are some common themes:

- Save more and save now.

- Maximize your RRSP contributions.

- Dump your guaranteed investment certificates.

- Buy mutual funds, specifically equity funds.

- Use a financial adviser. Don't do it yourself.

- Take out an investment loan, so your interest is tax-deductible.

None of these are bad rules. But speakers and sponsors tend to treat them as universal laws. That's dangerous. When the audience consists of up to 1,000 people attracted by newspaper ads and flyers, blanket advice is inappropriate. You have to account for varying levels of investing experience and risk tolerance.

Under Canada's securities law, investment dealers can't give the same advice to anyone who walks in the door. They have to follow a "know your client" rule, meaning they tailor what they say to individual needs and circumstances.

But financial seminars are exempt from the rules. Speakers don't have to be licensed or regulated and don't even need any financial planning credentials. They just have to be willing to tell you what to do with your money.

The things they tell you to do—saving more money, maximizing your RRSP and buying equity funds—will enrich the sponsoring financial adviser. Such advice also helps the mutual fund management companies, which pay up to half the cost of these seminars. So it's rare that you hear a good word for GICs, since financial advisers either don't sell them or make razor-thin commissions on them.

By the same token, it's common to hear about the wonders of leverage. Mortgaging your house and using the money to buy mutual funds can be a good plan if you're middle-aged, want to retire soon and haven't saved a nickel. But it also earns financial advisers a much bigger commission.

Leverage was something I just couldn't endorse. Nor could I push people to meet with the sponsoring adviser if they weren't interested. And I couldn't stop saying nice things about GICs, at least as part of a balanced portfolio. So my sideline career on the seminar circuit fizzled.

Duff Young, a licensed adviser and author who runs a firm called Fundmonitor.com, used to speak at 100 financial seminars a year. He says a few people told him they went for a free one-hour consultation and felt coerced to move their account over to the sponsor.

As a seminar speaker, Young tried to ask sponsors about their philosophy. For example, did they approve of taking out loans for investing?

One firm said it approved of loans in special cases. When Young arrived at the seminar, he found a loan application on everyone's seat. Shocked, he asked what was going on. The sponsor said everyone in the audience was likely to own a home. This made them all candidates for home equity loans, which they could use for investing.

Young, too, preferred not to do business with firms that pushed clients too heavily into leveraged investments. Borrowing to invest is suitable only for more experienced investors.

Until there are tougher rules for seminar speakers, here are some ways to protect yourself:

- Ask how the speaker is being paid and by whom.

- Find out if the speaker has a financial interest in the investments or the financial advisers he or she recommends.

- Check out the sponsoring firm thoroughly before transferring your money.

- Even if a speaker gives conservative investment advice, don't assume the sponsoring firm will take the same low-key approach.

- If a speaker recommends a tax shelter, find out if the write-offs have been approved by the Canada Customs and Revenue Agency and ask for a letter confirming it.

part four

Investing Money

Fifty-one per cent of Canadians now own stocks or equity mutual funds. Investing has become a mainstream activity, no longer confined to the affluent and elderly. Today, even children have investment portfolios and follow the markets.

There's a growing awareness that you can't keep all your money in guaranteed deposits. You won't have enough for your long-term goals, such as retirement or kids' post-secondary education, unless you take more risk. Stocks are the only investment with the potential to outpace inflation and taxes.

But you won't be a successful investor unless you're prepared to lose money. Equity investments can plummet in value in the short term and cause you great distress. Fads can be hard to resist. Only a few investors managed to avoid "the tech wreck" and "the dot bombs."

Experience makes losses more tolerable. You see your investments rise and fall and rise again, teaching you to be patient and take a long-term view. You learn (at least I did) not to watch too closely. Checking prices every day can make you crazy.

In this section, I'll talk about how to keep your emotions under control. One way is to put your investments on autopilot, so you're contributing the same amount of money through good markets and bad. You should understand why you're investing and how much growth you need to fulfill your objectives.

Next, we'll look at stocks and how they work. What's the difference between common and preferred shares? How do you figure out the dividend yield? Is it better to buy growth stocks or value stocks?

If you buy stocks, you must go through a broker. I'll give you guidelines on choosing a broker and questions to ask about safeguarding your investments. Do you want a full-service broker who offers advice, or a discount broker who simply takes your orders and executes them? That's a decision you'll have to make.

Then, we'll move on to bonds and explain why bond prices fall when interest rates rise (and vice versa). This seesaw relationship is a mystery to many Canadians, who only have experience with fixed-price Canada Savings Bonds or provincial savings bonds. And I'll look at whether you're better off investing in bonds or in bond funds.

Mutual funds are the next topic of discussion. I'll look at how you narrow down your choices among thousands of funds, and the different costs you pay when buying and selling funds. Another question to consider: How many funds are enough?

We'll close the section by looking at the wealth of information for investors in cyberspace. I'm not advocating that you get hooked up to the Internet to check your portfolio every hour. But I do think you're missing out on valuable resources, such as glossaries and commentaries, if you're not online. I'll point you to the best Web sites for increasing your investment savvy.

Get a handle on your emotions when investing

How much risk can you take? This is one of the toughest questions in investing. You may think you're comfortable with stock market volatility. At least, that's what you tell your financial adviser. You promise you won't panic when markets fluctuate and you lose money. But then it happens. After a sudden slump, your investments fall well below what you paid for them. The risk is no longer abstract, but terribly real.

You can't stop thinking about how much money you've lost. You feel queasy when you pick up a newspaper or hear a stock market report. You toss and turn in bed at night, wondering if your investments will ever recover.

Now you know the truth. You're less comfortable with volatility than you thought you were. Welcome to the club.

"Risk tolerance is socially acceptable, but most of us are less tolerant of risk than we want to let on," says George Hartman, a Vancouver-based financial consultant.

"When markets get crazy, people have a much greater temptation to stray from their long-term investment strategy."

In order to stick to a plan, you need to understand your emotional responses to risk. Here's a test to help you decide what kind of investor you are. It shows the factors to consider when deciding how much risk to take.

Stage of life

    (a)   I'm self-dependent and don't support anybody.

    (b)   I have dependents and other means of financial support.

    (c)   I have dependents and no other financial support.

    (d)   I'm near retirement.

    (e)   I'm retired.

Investment knowledge:

    (a)   Poor.

    (b)   Average.

    (c)   Good.

    (d)   Excellent.

Income needs:

    (a)   Current expenses not funded by investment income.

    (b)   Up to 10 per cent funded by investment income.

    (c)   11 to 25 per cent funded by investment income.

    (d)   26 to 50 per cent funded by investment income.

Expectations:

    (a)   My future earnings will far outpace inflation.

    (b)   They will stay marginally ahead of inflation.

    (c)   They will keep pace with inflation.

    (d)   They will decrease over time.

Temperament:

    (a)   I want low steady returns, with safety of principal at all times.

    (b)   I want medium returns, with a temporary decline in

principal at times.

(c)   I want above average returns and I'm prepared for fluctuations.

(d)   I want high returns with high risk.

Time horizon:

I plan to hold my investments for:

(a)   Three to six months.

(b)   Six months to eighteen months.

(c)   Eighteen months to four years.

(d)   Longer than four years.

Actions:

If my investment dropped 25 per cent in value, I would:

(a)   Sell it.

(b)   Sell part of it.

(c)   Do nothing.

(d)   Buy more of the same investment.

Leverage:

Would I borrow money to invest in a stock headed for stardom?

(a)   Definitely no.

(b)   May consider it.

(c)   Definitely yes.

Risk assessment tests such as this are a useful tool, helping you give accurate answers about your comfort with volatility. Your financial adviser should give you a risk test before filling out your client profile. If not, ask for one. Or fill out the test I gave you, so you can show it to an adviser you're thinking of hiring.

Once you know what kind of investor you are, stay within your comfort zone. Don't take on more risk than you can handle. You'll get too nervous and sell prematurely. That's a recipe for failure.

Losing money is never pleasant, but your ability to stomach risk improves with experience. It also helps to have a supportive spouse, friend or adviser to get you through the bad patches.

What are the psychological attributes of successful investors? These investors are courageous and cunning, with the confidence to buck the crowd and defy conventional wisdom. Here's a list from Richard Geist, president of the Institute of Psychology and Investing in Boston:

- They know they will make mistakes, but the mistakes don't threaten their self-esteem.

- They don't berate themselves or blame others.

- They change direction quickly, understand where they went wrong and tend not to make the same mistake again.

- They are confident about their ability to make decisions. A strong belief in their own intellectual capacities keeps them unshakeably optimistic.

- They stay slightly aloof from market fluctuations.

- They use a certain amount of denial when studying the media headlines, markets and stock prices.

- They establish strong bonds with another person while investing.

- They think of themselves as outsiders, not quite fitting in. This gives them the strength not to succumb to a herd mentality.

Go through the list and see where your weaknesses lie. Maybe you're too self-critical, unwilling to forget or forgive your errors. Maybe you're overly pessimistic, giving undue credibility to every gloomy economic report. Everyone has areas that need improvement.

I have trouble thinking long-term, since I work for a daily news-paper. I often confuse a temporary blip with a real trend.

The Y2K crisis, for example, really had me worried for a while. I thought the economy would dip when companies threw out other projects to fix their computers and software before Jan. 1, 2000. But the catastrophe predicted by the media never materialized.

Now that I recognize my weakness, I've learned a way to deal with it. Instead of worrying about what happens next month or next year, I try to think ahead to the year 2015 or 2020, when I'll be a senior citizen living on the money that is now invested.

There's always a short-term crisis. Today I'm worried about a possible U.S. war against Iraq, which could cripple the economy for a year or two. It doesn't look good for my investments.

But then, I imagine it's 2020 and I'm looking back at the crisis of 2002 or 2003. The war is long over and the economy is going strong. My investments not only have recovered, but they've also grown substantially.

By reminding myself that investing is a long-term game, I manage to live with political and stock market risk. I hang onto my portfolio without being constantly tempted to sell everything and hold only cash.

Another trick is to think about the different kinds of risk. Market risk is a threat if you're saving for a near-term goal. Suppose you plan to buy a house in three years, using money from your RRSP as a down payment. To minimize market risk, you invest in money market funds or term deposits.

But if you have a long-term goal, inflation risk is more insidious. This is the chance you won't make enough on your investments to out-pace taxes and the cost of living.

To reduce inflation risk, you want something with a higher return than money market funds and term deposits can provide. You invest in stocks and equity funds, knowing you have 10, 20 or even 30 years to ride out the occasional stock market slumps.

Put your investments on autopilot

Markets go up, markets go down. What's the best time to invest?

Ideally, you get into stocks when they're undervalued and get out when they're fully valued. That's the "buy low, sell high" approach.

But there's no rear-view mirror in investing. It's not hard to spot market trends in hindsight, but few of us can do it in real time. Even professional money managers often make the wrong decisions.

Market timers have to make two correct guesses: when to get out and when to get back in. The tough part is figuring out when to return. No one rings a bell to tell you when you can safely get in again.

The legendary investors with the great reputations, such as Warren Buffett and Sir John Templeton, pick stocks and stick with them. Good markets or bad, they're always invested. They don't build up cash when they see trouble coming.

You can follow their example by adopting a no-fuss strategy known as dollar cost averaging. I prefer using more evocative terms, such as autopilot or cruise control. Here's how it works:

- You put a fixed amount of money into mutual funds on a regular basis. If you can save $3,000 a year, you divide it into 12 amounts of $250 each or 24 amounts of $125 each.

- You automatically get more fund units with a fixed-dollar investment when markets fall and fewer units when markets rise.

- You think of market declines as an opportunity, not a threat, since your investment capital is going further. It's like loading up on tuna when the price drops to 99 cents a can from $1.50.

- You can invest more aggressively than you might have done before, since dollar cost averaging works well with highly volatile equity funds.

- If you're risk-averse, you can keep most of your money in a GIC and use the interest to buy fund units. Your capital is intact, but you get a possibly higher return through regular equity investment.

When you put your car on cruise control, you can sit back and relax and watch the scenery. The same thing happens when you set up a systematic purchase plan. You can ignore the stock market ups and downs and focus on more important things in your life.

Regular investing makes it easier to save and to stay the course in tough times. But it won't give you a higher return than lump sum investing. If someone tells you that, it's an exaggeration.

Let's say you invest $6,000 at the beginning of the year. You buy fund units at $10 each and they're worth $15 at the end of the year. By investing your money all at once, you get a return of 50 per cent.

But when you buy slowly each month, you're getting fund units at $11, $12, $13 and so on. There's an investment penalty since you're not in the market with all your capital from the beginning of the year.

Stocks go up more often than they go down. To say it another way, bull markets last longer than bear markets. That's why lump sum investing is generally a more profitable strategy. With dollar cost averaging, the extra fund units you buy when the price dips won't make up for the smaller amounts you get when the price rises.

If you adopt a dollar-cost averaging strategy, you might want to buy a fund that tracks a specific stock market index, such as the

S&P/TSX 60 or the Standard & Poor's 500 index. This is a low-cost way to invest and helps you avoid problems with superstar managers flaming out or leaving to go elsewhere. For more on index funds, see page 198.

Buy stocks with dividend reinvestment plans

If you want a low-cost way to buy stocks, look for companies that offer a dividend reinvestment plan (or DRIP). Shareholders who opt to join these plans no longer get a dividend cheque each quarter. Instead, their payments are used to buy additional shares in the company.

There are about 30 companies with DRIPs that trade on the Toronto Stock Exchange, mainly blue-chip firms like banks and utilities. Many of these companies also offer share purchase plans (or SPPs), which let you put in extra cash each quarter to buy more shares.

Companies with DRIPs and SPPs buy shares in the open market under the direction of a trustee. For them, it's a way to raise money without the expense of issuing new shares.

Because your shares are bought on a regular basis, you benefit from dollar-cost averaging. This lessens the risk of investing a large amount in a single investment at the wrong time.

A DRIP portfolio can yield high returns. That's the conclusion of Jim Otar, an independent financial adviser in Toronto and author of *Commission-Free Investing: Handbook of Canadian DRIPs and SPPs* (Uphill Publishing).

Otar invested a total of $1,000, divided equally among six companies, in June 1990. Twelve years later, the DRIP portfolio's value was $5,105. The compound annual return was 14.6 per cent, compared to 10.7 per cent for the average dividend fund and 9.2 per cent for the average Canadian equity fund.

"As of May 30, 2002, only one diversified Canadian equity mutual fund outperformed my portfolio consistently," Otar wrote in *Canadian MoneySaver* magazine. That fund, ABC Fundamental Value, has a $150,000 minimum investment.

You can expect a DRIP portfolio to do better than mutual funds because of the lower cost. Instead of paying management fees and expenses of 2 to 2.5 per cent a year to a fund manager, you're buying company shares for free.

Otar's basket of DRIPs, which he adjusted periodically to account for mergers, also outperformed the Toronto Stock Exchange 300 index. The TSE's compound annual return in the 12-year period was 9.6 per cent.

Dale Ennis, editor of *Canadian MoneySaver*, also invests in DRIPs and SPPs. He considers the strategy a "no-brainer," since he buys only reputable blue-chip companies and spends just an hour or two a month watching his portfolio.

Ennis, however, isn't a fan of dollar cost averaging. He likes to time his additional stock purchases so that he's buying at or near the 52-week low.

In the United States, DRIP investors can buy the first shares directly from the company. But in Canada, you generally have to buy the first shares through a brokerage firm and have them registered in your name. Even if you use a discount broker, you will pay a commission of $30 to $35 to buy shares and $25 or more to register them in your name.

If you already own the company's shares, you will have to reregister them in your name. "Ask your broker to do so," Ennis advises. "Probably you'll face resistance, as he will no longer profit from your future purchases."

You can find a primer on DRIPs and SPPs at the Web site www.canadianmoneysaver.ca. If you want names and details on the companies offering these plans, you have to subscribe to the magazine. The cost is $21.35 a year for the print or online editions.

Buy stocks as an inflation hedge

You may think the only investment risk is losing money when markets tank. But you're exposed to risk even when your capital is guaranteed. Inflation risk is the loss of purchasing power when your investment returns don't keep up with the cost of living.

Stock ownership is a way to guard against inflation risk. When you invest in a stock, you buy a piece of a company and participate in its long-term growth. A well-run company should generate returns that exceed the cost of living.

Is it better to buy individual stocks or stock mutual funds? You're a candidate for mutual funds if you don't have enough money ($25,000 or more) to buy a diversified portfolio of stocks.

Funds are also better if you want a low-maintenance investment. You don't have to research companies and read their quarterly reports. And you don't have keep an eye on the stock market to decide when to buy and sell.

But stocks are more fun. You watch the price move up. You see the stock split two for one. Suddenly your 500 shares become 1,000. Your money doubles or triples in a few months, while mutual funds chug along gaining 10 to 15 per cent a year. At that rate, it will take you five to seven years to double your money.

"It's that psychological reward of picking a winner that motivates so many investors to set aside mutual funds and test their hands in the stock market," say Lori Bamber and Gene Walden in *The 50 Best Stocks for Canadians* (John Wiley & Sons).

Another benefit of stock ownership is the freedom to make your own choices. If you're a socially conscious investor, you can avoid putting money into businesses you dislike, such as tobacco, alcohol or gambling.

Yes, there are mutual funds that take a socially conscious approach. But when you invest in them, you're letting someone else decide the fate of your money. You may not agree with all of the fund manager's ideals.

But here's something you should never forget: Buying individual stocks exposes you to more market risk than buying funds. Companies can suffer big losses when new competitors arrive or management turns sour. Former blue chips turn into penny stocks (Nortel Networks) or stop trading altogether (Laidlaw Inc).

If you own shares in a company that goes under, you're last in line (after the tax authorities, employees and creditors) to make a claim on its assets. You stand to lose everything you invested.

With a mutual fund, it's rare—almost unheard of—to lose everything you invested. There's enough diversification that the winners offset the losers.

It's important to distinguish between common shares and preferred shares. Both shares represent ownership in a company, but common shares give more voting rights. If the company is insolvent and has to liquidate assets, any money left over after the creditors are paid goes to the preferred shareholders first, then to common shareholders.

Preferred share investors are usually promised a fixed dividend forever. This is unlike common shares, whose dividends are variable and never guaranteed. Preferred shares are more stable than common shares, since their prices move in tandem with interest rates. Common shares are more risky, but the upside is that they usually outperform preferred shares in the long run.

Diversified stock investors will hold a mix of growth stocks and value stocks. If you're more aggressive and you like to gamble on a company's potential, growth is your style. If you're more conservative and you like bargains, value will suit you better.

Value is one of the oldest ways to pick stocks. Your best introduction is *The Intelligent Investor* (HarperCollins) by U.S. finance professor Benjamin Graham, first published in 1949 and still in print. With a new foreword by Warren Buffett, the book is a bestseller at the Amazon.com and Amazon.ca Web sites.

Graham is responsible for the fact that investors even think about things like the price/earnings ratio. He studied the stock market crash of 1929 and tried to find rules investors could use to get safe, sustainable and market-beating results.

The P/E ratio helps you decide whether a stock is undervalued or overvalued. You can work it out yourself by dividing the stock's current price by the company's current annual earnings per share.

If you see analysts quoting a higher P/E ratio than the one you calculate, they're not using earnings from the last four quarters (the trailing P/E ratio). They may be working from estimates of the earnings expected in the next four quarters (the projected P/E ratio). Or they may take the sum of the last two actual quarters' earnings and the estimates of the next two quarters' earnings.

Value investing doesn't mean buying a stock just because it's cheap. A low P/E ratio may be a sign of something fundamentally wrong with a company or sector. Telecommunications stocks, for example, tumbled in price because of industry overcapacity. Investors who thought they saw value lost money with each profit shortfall.

Growth stocks often have no earnings and no P/E ratio. They're more volatile than the stock market as a whole. For growth investors, the trend is what counts. Even a money-losing company may have positive momentum if its losses are shrinking each year.

While established firms may have 10 to 12 per cent average annual increases in earnings, growth companies can increase their earnings by 20 per cent a year. But it's important to remember that outstanding earnings growth is a short-term phenomenon.

Few companies can sustain a 20 per cent profit pattern year in and year out. Today's growth stock may be tomorrow's blue chip, with profit increases in the 10 to 12 per cent range. That's not necessarily a bad thing, because blue-chip stocks pay dividends.

Dividends are cash payments to stockholders that come out of company profits. They're usually paid every three months. Only mature and stable companies pay dividends. Younger companies reinvest profits in the business to sustain their growth. (Don't confuse stock dividends with insurance company dividends, which are actually a refund of overpaid premiums.)

You can find the dividend yield in newspapers' stock listings. To work it out yourself, divide the company's annual dividends by the share price.

Here's an example. Common shares of the Canadian Imperial Bank of Commerce pay annual dividends of $1.64. The stock was trading at $42.35 (in early September 2002), so the dividend yield was 3.9 per cent ($1.64 divided by $42.35).

In terms of income, 3.9 per cent is a good deal. It's twice what you could earn on a one-year guaranteed investment certificate from CIBC. But the dividend yield was higher than usual because the share price was down from a 52-week high of $58.04.

Bank stocks are suitable for conservative investors. So are utility stocks, which provide high dividend yields of three to five per cent. They have strong, secure revenues from power, gas or telephone operations, which they pass through to shareholders. Utilities are known as defensive stocks. No matter how bad the economy, people keep their homes warm and light and connected with others.

When comparing stock dividends with the income from GICs and bonds, you can't ignore taxes. Companies pay tax on their profits before distributing dividends, so the money is not fully taxed in the investor's hands. You get to keep more money in your pocket.

A payment of $1,000 in dividends from a taxable Canadian company is worth $775 after tax if you're in the middle tax bracket (earning $30,000 to $60,000 of taxable income). But with $1,000 in interest from GICs or bonds, you get to keep only $600 to $640.

The favourable tax treatment makes a difference if you hold stocks outside a registered retirement savings plan. Dividend income has no tax advantage inside an RRSP, since all withdrawals are taxed at the highest marginal rate.

Test drive your broker before signing up

If you buy stocks on your own, and not through a mutual fund, you have to work with a stockbroker. How much service do you want? That's your first decision.

Full-service brokers offer their own stock research and access to a broad range of investment products. They call themselves a variety of names: investment executives, financial advisers or financial consultants.

You pay a higher commission rate with a full-service broker than with a discount broker. But full-service brokers negotiate commissions and cut them in some circumstances, such as when you're buying shares for a child.

Discount brokers offer the same products as full-service firms. But the commission costs are lower, since you do your own research and place your own orders. The people you deal with don't provide advice but act as order takers. They're compensated by salary.

Many investors have trading accounts at both full-service and discount brokers and divide their business according to how much help they need and how much they want to pay.

Do you want to trade online? That's your second decision.

When comparing online brokers, you can check out the rankings at www.gomez.com and www.moneysense.ca. Both Web sites test the services provided by Canadian brokerage firms and publish numerical scores.

Gomez Inc. gives the top score to BMO InvestorLine, followed by TD Waterhouse and E*Trade Canada. MoneySense's survey found the best online brokerage was Charles Schwab Canada, which was later taken over by the Bank of Nova Scotia.

You also can do your own service measurements. Start by calling discount brokers to ask for literature and see how long it takes to reach a live person.

Call the toll-free customer help line with a prepared question. See how long you are left on hold and how many people you have to speak to before getting the answer you want.

Send a message via the Web site and see how long it takes the broker to respond to your email.

Do you want your trades checked for suitability? That's your third decision.

If, in the interests of speedier service, you decide to let your broker out of this requirement, you will have to sign a disclaimer saying you know you're taking risks and you're responsible if anything goes wrong.

You need to be sure of your research and trading skills before signing such a disclaimer. Think about getting independent legal or financial advice, advises Sandra Foster in *Who's Minding Your Money?* (John Wiley & Sons).

Online investing is cheaper but there are also risks. It's easy to do too much trading and the costs add up. You're responsible for the tax reporting of your capital gains and losses. You have to sort out the good research from the bad. And you may trade in markets where there aren't enough buyers and sellers.

Investment mediator Robert Goldin has seen many beginners trading online without knowing what they're doing. Investing in initial public offerings can be especially risky if the shares go up quickly in value.

Goldin had a client who bought into an initial public offering of Palm Inc. The day before the shares began trading, when the price was set at $38 (U.S.), she placed an online order to be filled at the market price. Palm shares, traded on the Nasdaq Stock Market, were in heavy demand and quickly soared to $145. She ended up with 280 shares at $136.75 each. Total cost: $38,290 (U.S.), twice the cash she had in her trading account.

To cover the debt in her account, the broker sold her shares for $67 each, leaving her to cover a loss of about $30,000 (Canadian). She could have saved herself the grief if she had put in an order that set a price limit.

Without getting advice, many investors don't understand the dangers of buying volatile stocks or initial stock offerings on margin (that is, with borrowed money) and how quickly they can be wiped out.

The suitability rules are there for your protection. They ensure that a broker double-checks your trades if they fall outside your comfort zone and asks if you understand what you're doing. Only sophisticated investors should apply for an exemption.

A few things to ask your broker

Herschel, a *Toronto Star* reader, had bought $8,000 worth of junior mining stocks through Buckingham Securities Corp. of Toronto. He was distressed when the Ontario Securities Commission put an indefinite trading ban on the brokerage firm, because of a capital shortfall of at least $1 million.

Buckingham had 14 salespeople and 2,400 clients. But the firm was not a Toronto Stock Exchange member and did all its trading through other brokerages. It had margin accounts with at least seven Bay Street brokerage firms and was holding clients' assets in these accounts.

Brokers are legally required to keep securities paid for by clients in separate accounts. It's against the law to mix up assets belonging to investors with assets owned by the brokerage firm.

The provincial securities regulator stepped in because of a concern that brokers would use assets owned by Buckingham clients as security for the money they were owed on the margin accounts. "I never dreamed that someone else would be doing the trading," says Herschel, a client for two years.

He got involved with Buckingham because he knew a salesperson and acted on a few of his recommendations. He didn't investigate the firm before it collapsed.

He's not alone. Few investors understand they can protect themselves by asking a few questions of a brokerage firm:

- Are you a member of the Investment Dealers Association of Canada? Brokerage firms must belong to a self-regulating organization. IDA members generally have high capital levels and good records. To check out member firms, go to www.ida.ca or call 416-364-6133.

- Do you have affiliates that are regulated differently? This is fairly common. Assante Capital Management Ltd. is an IDA member, for example, while Assante Financial Management Ltd. is not an IDA member. Since Assante Financial Management is a mutual fund dealer, it's part of a new self-regulatory organization, the Mutual Fund Dealers Association (MFDA).

- Are you a member of the Canadian Investor Protection Fund (CIPF)? All IDA member firms also belong to the CIPF, which protects investors' assets when an investment dealer is insolvent. It does not cover stock market losses. Investors are covered for up to $1 million in securities and cash in general accounts, and can claim up to $1 million more for assets in registered plans, joint accounts, personal holding companies and trusts. To check out member firms, go to www.cipf.ca. Buckingham clients were not covered by the CIPF.

- Do you belong to one of the major stock exchanges? Does your firm do its own trading or does it work through intermediaries?

There are about 60,000 financial advisers in Canada who sell mutual funds and work for firms that are not IDA members. That's why securities regulators set up the Mutual Fund Dealers Association. Fund dealers had to join either the IDA or the MFDA by June 2002.

The MFDA plans to set up a $5 million investor protection fund, financed by member firms, by July 1, 2003. Investors will be covered for up to $100,000 each. This is less than the $1 million coverage for IDA member firms under the Canadian Investor Protection Fund.

Why are there two levels of protection? MFDA member firms generally hold investments in the client's name. These assets are held in a trust account, segregated from the firm's day-to-day operations, and are not distributed to creditors if the firm goes under.

IDA member firms hold investments in the firm's name, also known as nominee name or "street name." They're required to segregate securities if clients have paid for them in full, but they're allowed to use clients' cash for other purposes. This privilege is spelled out in the account agreement. Here's what one IDA member tells clients: "Any monies held from time to time to the client's credit need not be segregated and may be used in the ordinary conduct of the firm's business."

IDA dealers are allowed to do underwriting, principal and margin trading activities that expose them to extra risk. They are more likely to go bankrupt than MFDA dealers.

If an IDA firm goes bankrupt, clients' assets are exposed because the firm has assumed legal ownership. That's why the CIPF offers $1 million of insolvency coverage to investors, while the MFDA plans to limit it to $100,000.

When buying mutual funds, you can protect yourself by making your cheque payable to the mutual fund manager. Don't make it payable to the MFDA member firm. This will safeguard your money if the fund dealer goes under before passing it along to the mutual fund manager.

Buy bonds for income and stability

Rodney Dangerfield's famous line, "I don't get no respect," applies to bonds. They're a low-profile investment that few people understand. And they rarely rate a mention in the media, even though Canada's bond market is many times bigger than its stock market.

Bonds provide regular income and give stability to a portfolio. While less volatile than stocks, bonds have given Canadian investors almost as high returns in recent decades. Your own asset allocation will depend on your comfort with risk and the level of interest rates.

First, let's dispel a misconception. The Canada Savings Bond is not actually a bond, but a short-term savings certificate issued by the federal government. Provincial governments also issue savings bonds. Unlike other bonds, savings bonds don't fluctuate in price. They can be cashed at full face value, plus earned interest, during their term.

But there's one thing that Canada Savings Bonds have in common with other bonds: The buyers are lending money to a government, a crown corporation or a business enterprise. In return, they get what is essentially an IOU, except it's called a bond or debenture.

A bond's par value (in most cases) is $100. This is what the borrower promises to pay you when the bond matures on a specific date in the future. But you're not lending money for free, so the borrower must also pay you a premium or "coupon" at a set interest rate every six months until maturity.

Here's an example of how the bond market works:

- In 1998, you bought a bond, due September 1, 2004. It has a coupon of 8 per cent, paying $4 for each $100 face value of March 1 and September 1 of each year.

- If you hold the bond until it matures on September 1, 2004, you will have no capital gain or loss. You bought the bond at par and it will be paid off at par.

- If interest rates rise to 10 per cent shortly after the bond is issued, the 8 per cent coupon is less attractive. So you can buy the bond at a discount from the $100 par value—say $94. You get the same income, $8 for each $100 face value, but you also get a capital gain of $6 over six years (or $1 a year). Your annual return is now $9. Divide $9 by $94 (the bond price) and your yield is 9.57 per cent.

- The same thing works in reverse. If interest rates fall to 6 per cent, you will have to pay a higher price for an 8 per cent bond, say $106. If you hold the bond to maturity, you will get only $100. This means you have a capital loss of $5. Your annual return is now $7. Divide $7 by $106 and your yield is 6.6 per cent.

- You can opt to sell your bond in the market at any time. If interest rates go down and the bond's value goes up, you can sell at a premium. If interest rates rise and you have to sell at a discount, you may want to hold the bond to maturity. However, your return will never be lower than the coupon on the bond.

Since bonds rise in value when interest rates fall, some people time their purchases to earn capital gains. They buy bonds when interest rates are high and sell them when rates drop. The classic time to buy bonds is when economic growth slows down and central banks cut interest rates to ward off a recession.

To buy bonds, you must have an account with an investment dealer. (Some discount brokers offer online bond trading). You also need an initial investment of at least $5,000 and up to $25,000.

Stripped bonds, known as "strips" in Canada and "zero coupon bonds" in the United States, are a popular investment. They're created when a dealer buys a large bond from a government or corporation and strips away the coupons for each semiannual interest payment.

You buy strips at a discounted price. The longer to go until maturity, the less you'll pay. The difference between today's purchase price and the value at maturity is expressed as an annual yield.

Say, for example, you buy a bond on September 1, 2002. The maturity date is September 1, 2006. You will pay $85.18 for the bond and you will receive $100 four years later. The yield is 4.05 per cent.

Since strips don't pay annual interest, they're more volatile than regular bonds and can swing wildly in value as rates move up and down. If rates drop, you can earn big capital gains by selling them before maturity. You should hold strips only in a tax-sheltered plan such as an RRSP or registered retirement income fund (RRIF). Otherwise, you'll be taxed on the imputed annual interest, money you haven't received and that won't be in your hands for many years.

"With strips, there are no surprises," says author Gordon Pape. "If you're planning to retire in 15 years, you simply buy 15-year strips when interest rates are high, tuck them away in your RRSP and forget them. The money will be there when you need it."

Here are other investments that fall into the fixed-income category:

- **Callable bonds**. They can be redeemed, or "called," by the issuer before they mature, usually for a stated price and at a particular time. When you're buying a bond, check whether it is callable and, if so, when and where. And watch the financial press, so you won't expect interest to be paid on a bond that's been redeemed.

- **Foreign-currency bonds**. Canadian governments and corporations often issue bonds denominated in foreign currencies, such as U.S. dollars, Japanese yen, British pounds sterling or euros. They count as Canadian content for RRSP purposes and also provide diversification. If you strongly believe the Canadian dollar is about to plunge, you may want to consider them.

- **Real-return bonds**. Launched in 1991 by the federal government when the inflation rate was 4.5 per cent, these bonds guarantee to pay a certain amount over the increase in the consumer price index. If you feel inflation is a threat, real-return bonds provide a hedge. You can hold them individually or through the TD Real-Return Bond Fund.

- **Mortgage-backed securities**. These are shares in a pool of residential first mortgages, guaranteed by the Canada Mortgage and Housing Corp. Payments are made monthly, which suits retirees and others living on the income. Each payment is a blend of principal and interest.

- **Convertible bonds**. Issued by corporations, convertibles combine the fixed interest rate and maturity date of a bond with the capital gains potential of a stock. Investors have the right to convert these bonds into common shares at stated prices over stated periods. Convertible bonds appeal to people who are willing to accept a lower bond yield in return for a chance to profit in the growth of the company's shares.

- **Royalty income trusts**. You're buying a share of a mature business enterprise, which pays most of its income to investors. The cash flow depends on the success of the underlying business. Royalty trusts are popular when interest rates are low, since they pay higher yields and often have tax advantages. But there's no maturity date or principal amount to be repaid, so you can also have capital losses.

Let's face it: Bonds are complicated, and there's an extraordinary range of choices. This is why most investors buy bond funds. They like having a professional manager on their side to sort through the choices and decide what suits the current economic climate.

Another problem is lack of transparency. When you buy stocks, the broker's commission is shown clearly on the confirmation statement. But with bonds, the commission is built into the price of the bond itself. Unless you can find the same bond at another brokerage house, you will never know exactly what you're paying in service fees.

Costs are more visible when you buy bond funds. The management fees and expenses run at an average 1 to 1.5 per cent a year. They take a big bite of your return when interest rates on bonds are only 4 to 5 per cent.

But there are low-cost alternatives in the bond fund world. The Phillips, Hager & North Bond Fund, a top performer, charges a below-average 0.6 per cent a year. Another winner is the McLean Budden Fixed Income Fund, which has annual fees of 0.7 per cent.

You can also buy low-cost bond index funds from TD Canada Trust, Canadian Imperial Bank of Commerce, Royal Bank and Bank of Nova Scotia. These funds, which are easier to manage since they simply track an index, have annual fees of less than one per cent a year.

However, there's one reason why you may be able to do better investing directly in bonds, rather than in bond funds.

A bond has a maturity date. You know you will get the face value if you hold the bond until it matures. But there's no guaranteed return of capital with bond funds, since there's no maturity date.

When bond funds first became popular, many buyers thought the their investments would go up in value when interest rates went up.

They were shocked to find they lost money with rising rates, since their lower-yielding bonds were marked down in price.

If you're a buy-and-hold investor, you will probably make money with either bonds or bond funds over long periods. But if you have to sell unexpectedly, you're better off buying individual bonds.

How to pick mutual funds

Mutual funds are one of the great inventions of the twentieth century. They give people of modest means easy access to investments that were once limited to the rich.

I consider myself lucky as a journalist to have had a front-row seat at the show. I started covering mutual funds in 1987, when there were 500 funds with $20 billion in assets. The industry now manages more than $400 billion, spread among several thousand funds.

Here are the main arguments for buying mutual funds rather than investing directly in stocks, bonds and money market instruments:

- **Professional management**. It takes time and energy to watch the markets, buy at the right price and decide when to sell. With funds, you can hire an expert to make the investment decisions for you.

- **Diversification**. You need at least $25,000 to buy 10 blue-chip stocks in diverse sectors. With mutual funds, you can get such a portfolio for $500 to $1,000. You can diversify even further with funds that invest in foreign securities.

- **Liquidity**. Your money is not tied up and you can sell any time you want at the fund's current net asset value. You don't have to worry about finding a buyer for your securities.

- **Convenience**. After your initial investment in a fund, you can buy a little at a time by transferring money from a bank account. The fund manager keeps all the records for tax purposes and reinvests your distributions, too.

These are all legitimate arguments. That's why you hear them over and over again from fund sellers. But each reason has a flip side, a negative that you may not have considered.

Professional managers are good, but they're not infallible. Even superstars can misread the market and produce poor results. You have to watch carefully to see if the manager is still performing well and is still there. The pros have a nasty habit of moving around.

Diversification goes only so far in the Canadian stock market. If you own several funds, you may find they hold the same stocks. When Nortel Networks was riding high at $120 a share, I did a survey that showed 885 of 3,163 funds had Nortel among their top 10 holdings and 414 funds had Nortel as their top holding. Technology stocks were hot and many funds overloaded on them.

Liquidity can be an illusion when you face a hefty hit at the exit door. Most funds are sold with deferred sales charges, which vanish only after you've held on to your units for five or six years. And when you redeem, you often don't know what price you will get till the next business day.

Buying funds on the instalment plan is convenient and helps you deal with volatility. But you may get a lower return when you invest your money gradually, rather than investing a lump sum all at once.

Fund sellers have no basis to claim that dollar cost averaging will make you richer.

With more than 3,000 funds for sale in Canada, how do you narrow your search and find a fund that meets your needs?

Step One: Choose a strong manager and management firm. You want to switch easily if things don't work out as you had hoped.

Find an established parent company that offers at least a dozen fund choices in the major investment categories.

Step Two: **Read the prospectus**. This is a useful document that outlines in plain language the risks and costs of investing. Many people see the prospectus only after they've purchased. Make sure you get a copy while you still have time to cancel your order.

Step Three: **Look for consistent performance**. You're better off buying a fund that is always slightly above average than one with spectacular six-month or one-year results. Check the fund's performance against the appropriate benchmarks.

Step Four: **Find out the fund's investment style**. Is it growth, value, momentum, top-down, bottom-up or some combination of the above?

If you own several funds, you should try to diversify by style. Don't take the manager's word for it; do your own research. Read the marketing material and try to figure out which investment approach is having the most influence over the fund's performance.

Watch out for style drift. That happens when fund managers adopt styles that are currently in favour, rather than sticking with the style they started with. Good managers stick to their guns. If they have a strong tilt toward value, they don't desert their discipline to buy growth stocks.

Some managers are known as "closet indexers." They don't have a style (even if they say they do) and they build portfolios that simply track the market index. You can get the same results at a much lower cost by buying a true index fund.

How many funds do you need?

Mutual funds are popular because they add variety to a portfolio. But how much diversification is too much?

Financial advisers often see people who divvy up their RRSP contributions among the leading fund companies year after year. They own a hodgepodge of 30 to 40 mutual funds with overlapping content and investment styles.

"The client's investment collection is reminiscent of a tangle of Christmas lights," says John Hood of J.C. Hood Investment Counsel Inc. in Toronto, "with several varieties of equity funds, bond funds, labour-sponsored funds and emerging markets funds tossed together."

What is the minimum number of funds you need in order to cover all the bases? That depends on how much money you have available to invest.

You can get enough diversification with just two funds if you start with $1,000 or less. You should pick a Canadian balanced fund and an international balanced fund. Balanced funds are good for those with smaller amounts to invest. Your money is allocated among the three major asset classes (stocks, bonds and cash).

If you prefer to do your own asset allocation, you should own at least five funds: a Canadian and a global bond fund, plus Canadian, U.S. and global equity funds (one that invests outside North America).

These five funds cover all the bases, except cash. Money market funds can be expensive to own but there are other ways to hold cash, such as a bank account, short-term deposit or Canada Savings Bond. To diversify further, you can eliminate the global equity fund and divide your money among European, Japanese, Asian and emerging markets funds. That gives you eight funds altogether.

Are you a gambler? Do you love playing the market? If so, you may want to add another fund to the mix. Set aside a small amount to invest in something risky. Try your luck with a biotech fund, for example, or a global entertainment fund.

But don't go overboard. If you own too many funds, you end up with the same return as the stock market index. You can buy a low-cost index fund to get an index-like return. You don't have to pay higher annual fees for active management.

What's the magic number? It's five to 10 funds, says Ted Cadsby, author of *The Ten Biggest Investment Mistakes Canadians Make* (Stoddart). If you hold more than 10 funds, you're over diversified.

Altamira Financial Services Ltd., which sells funds directly to the public, caters to investors who start with as little as $50 a month. For those with $10,000 or more to invest, Altamira offers managed portfolios of five to 12 funds.

"We think 12 is probably the number you can have without being over diversified," says national sales manager Jason Grieve.

That rule applies even if you start with $50,000 or $100,000, Grieve insists. Once you go beyond a dozen funds, you face the danger of diluting your results.

How to save money buying funds

Mutual fund investors pay a number of different expenses. Let's go through them one by one and see how they can be reduced.

1. **Management expense ratio (MER)**. This is an annual fee charged to investors in the fund, which pays for portfolio management, administration, legal costs, marketing and advertising. The MER is deducted before the annual return is calculated and published.

2. **Sales charge**. This is a commission paid to the fund dealer in return for financial advice. Investors pay the sales charge in advance or when they sell the fund.

3. **Trading costs**. These are brokerage commissions and bid/ask spreads, paid by fund managers when they trade stocks and bonds. Trading costs are not included in the fund's MER. Funds with high portfolio turnover incur higher brokerage costs.

4. **Insurance fees**. These are added to the MER when you buy a segregated or protected fund that guarantees your principal. You pay 0.5 per cent to 1 per cent more each year for this insurance coverage.

5. **Wrap fees.** These may be paid to an adviser for selecting, monitoring and adjusting the allocation of funds within your account. They are usually applied on top of the MER.

6. **Taxes on distributions**. Fund managers earn interest and dividends on their securities, as well as capital gains when they sell stocks at a profit. You pay tax on the distributions they pass along to you, unless you hold your funds in a tax-sheltered retirement plan.

7. **Taxes on redemptions**. When you sell a fund that has gone up in value, you pay tax on your capital gain (on top of any capital gains taxes the manager has passed along to you in annual distributions). However, your gains are tax-sheltered inside a retirement savings plan.

8. **Trustee fees.** These are paid annually to the financial institution that holds your registered retirement savings plan.

Costs vary widely from one investor to another. Not everyone pays the same amount. But here's a handy rule of thumb, devised by actuary Malcolm Hamilton of Mercer Human Resource Consulting:

- Take the number 40.

- Add up your total annual expense rate and divide that number into 40.

- The result is the number of years it takes for expenses to consume one-third of your investment.

Suppose you own a fund with a two per cent MER. According to the rule of 40, you lose one-third of your investment to fees in 20 years.

MERs are usually the biggest cost for fund owners, but there are other annual expenses. Suppose, in addition to a two per cent MER, you also pay one per cent a year in trading costs and one per cent a year in taxes. The result: You lose one-third of your investment to expenses in 10 years.

Fund costs may look insignificant, but they add up. Try to keep them as low as possible. If funds have similar returns, pick the one with the lowest MER. Go through the prospectus, annual report, statements and tax slips to see what your other expenses are. Know what you're paying.

The prospectus has a section called "financial highlights" that shows the MER for the past few years. Find out if the MER is increasing, decreasing or staying the same. In general, costs should come down as a fund's assets go up (because of economies of scale).

Most investors choose funds with deferred sales charges (DSC) or back-end loads. There's no initial commission, but you pay up to five or six per cent on the way out if you sell within a few years. If your fund has a DSC, check to see how quickly it disappears and whether it's calculated on the amount you originally invested or the current market value. (You're better off with the market value in case you to dump a poor performer, while you're better off with the original investment if you're selling a winner.)

Find out if you can redeem up to 10 per cent of your fund units every year without sales charges. This is a way to get your money out sooner; most funds allow it. You can redeem up to 20 per cent quickly by making withdrawals in December and January.

Avoid DSCs if possible. They trap you into staying with funds that aren't performing, or they magnify your losses when you do leave. Either outcome is unpleasant.

If you have no alternative, make sure you pick a big fund family with many investment choices. That way, you can switch from one fund to another in the first few years without incurring a DSC.

Dealers also sell funds with a front-end load of two to three per cent, which comes off your original investment. Consider this instead of a DSC. Though you don't have all your money working for you right away, at least you're free to leave without worrying about an exit fee.

Some no-frills dealers sell funds without sales charges to gain a competitive edge. They still make money, since the fund manager pays them a "trailer fee" of 0.5 to 1 per cent a year that comes out of the management expense ratio. If you don't like sales charges, look for a broker or dealer who is willing to live off the trailer fees. When buying funds from a discount broker, watch out for redemption fees that kick in if you sell within the first three months.

Another choice you have is to buy funds that have no sales charges. Called no-load funds, they're available from banks, trust companies and fund managers that sell directly to the public (such as Altamira Investment Services, Phillips Hager & North, Sceptre Investment Counsel or Saxon Funds).

Don't assume that no-load funds have lower MERs than funds with sales charges. Banks, trust companies and direct sellers have high marketing budgets and also pay trailers to salespeople. Their no-load funds are often no bargains when it comes to total costs.

Luckily, there's an Internet tool that helps you see the impact of fund fees and expenses. Developed by the Ontario Securities Commission and Industry Canada, it's on both their Web sites (www.osc.gov.on.ca and www.consumerconnection.ic.gc.ca).

You enter the amount of your initial investment and how long you plan to hold it, along with the fund's sales charges and MER. Then you get a pie chart that shows the final value of the investment, along with total fees and foregone earnings.

Look at low-cost index funds

Indexing is a fast-growing investment strategy. The best way to define indexing, also known as passive management, is to contrast it to the more familiar approach to investing, active management.

Active managers choose certain stocks or bonds they believe will generate higher returns than other stocks or bonds. They're judged against other money managers and against an appropriate index, which is a statistical measure of the changes in a portfolio of stocks representing a portion of the overall market.

Passive managers don't do research, analyze companies' financial results and crunch numbers late into the night. Nor do they fly around the world interviewing company executives or checking out the newest mining technology. They simply buy all the securities included in an index and hold on to them.

"The active manager buys and sells with the view to generating better performance than the index, while a passive manager buys and holds to generate the same performance as an index," says Ted Cadsby, author of *The Power of Index Funds: Canada's Best-Kept Investment Secret* (Stoddart).

Here's why Cadsby likes the strategy:

- Very few managers consistently outperform the index over time.

- The managers who do outperform don't beat the index by much.

- Many of the managers who lag behind the index do so by a very wide margin.

- It's hard to pick the managers who will outperform. There's no consensus among the experts, and past winners often become losers.

- Index funds are more consistent and predictable.

There are about 100 index funds available to Canadian investors, a fraction of the 3,000 non-index funds sold here. They're not nearly as popular as in the United States.

Buying an index fund means accepting that there are no famous investors who can outperform year in and year out. It may be realism—but to many investors, it's pessimism.

Another reason index funds haven't taken off in Canada: There's no money in them for salespeople. Typically, these funds have low management fees (averaging 0.9 per cent, compared to 2.25 per cent for actively managed funds) and no front or back loads. Index funds are cheaper because the manager doesn't have to pick securities. And with the buy-and-hold nature of index investing, there's lower turnover and trading costs.

Commission-paid sellers have little incentive to plug index funds, since they do far better financially with actively managed funds. They have an interest in encouraging our faith in superstars. It means more business for them, as clients buy the rising stars and sell those that have waned.

Only the banks and one direct seller, Altamira Investment Services Inc., distribute index funds. Banks got into index funds originally for an odd reason.

"They didn't want to pay the competitive compensation packages the hero managers were earning in the 1980s at the independent fund companies," says financial writer Brian Noble in *The Index Investing Revolution* (Macmillan). Then banks looked at the index fund boom in the United States and concluded this style of investing made sense.

A newer type of index investment is the exchange-traded fund (ETF). When you buy an ETF, you're buying units of a trust that holds all the stocks in an index. ETFs trade on a stock exchange. You pay a standard commission to buy and sell them. You need a brokerage account to get involved.

Why trade ETFs when you can buy an index fund and pay no brokerage commissions? The advantage is lower ongoing management fees. The i60 units, which track the Standard & Poor's/TSX index, have an MER of 0.17 per cent. And SPDRs, which track the Standard & Poor's 500 index, have an MER of 0.12 per cent. You can get more information on the 11 ETFs marketed by Barclays Global Investors Canada at www.iunits.com.

"Core and explore" is an investment strategy that gives the best of both worlds. You put part of your portfolio in index funds (core) and part in actively managed funds (explore).

The index funds provide diversification, low costs and consistent performance. You won't beat the market and you won't lag behind, either. Tax efficiency is another advantage of index funds. They keep portfolio turnover low, which means fewer capital gains passed on to investors. Finally, index funds are transparent. You know exactly what you own.

The actively managed funds provide specialization, extra spice and the chance of earning better-than-index returns.

Research by Charles Schwab Corp., a big U.S. broker, shows that a core-and-explore portfolio runs less risk of lagging the market and has more potential to beat the market than an all-explore or all-core approach.

Beware of the year-end surprise

Taxes are an important consideration to anyone contemplating a mutual fund purchase at the end of the year. Certainly, you can get a nasty year-end surprise if you hold mutual funds outside a registered retirement savings plan.

By law, funds must pass along all interest and dividends and any realized capital gains, net of expenses, to investors each year. This usually happens in late December.

If you buy a fund just before the gains are distributed, the payout will be taxable in your hands. And most of it will represent income you haven't earned or received.

It may seem unfair, but you get the same year-end distribution no matter what time of year you buy the fund. This punishes people who buy a fund after it realizes most of its gains for the year.

I once heard from a *Toronto Star* reader who had an unexpectedly large mutual fund distribution. He complained so loudly that he won a refund from the fund manager.

Alan, a senior citizen, had invested almost $500,000 in the Royal U.S. Index Fund. He picked an index fund because it is not actively managed and normally produces little in the way of taxable capital gains. Tax efficiency was important to him. He didn't want his Old Age Security payments clawed back because his net income was too high.

Soon afterward, the Royal Bank introduced a new fund and asked Alan if he wanted to switch. The Royal U.S. Premium Index Fund, aimed at those with $250,000 or more to invest, had a razor-thin expense ratio of 0.3 per cent.

"I would have been better off if I had just stayed where I was," Alan told me, since his decision to switch triggered the problem.

A few large investors in the Royal Premium U.S. Index Fund suddenly withdrew their money in the spring of 2000. The assets shrank to $10 million, down from $24 million at the start of 2000.

The fund was forced to sell stocks at the market peak. As a result, it gave the remaining investors a distribution of $2.80 a unit (of which $2.57 was capital gains) in December 2000. This was many times richer than the payout of 9 cents a unit in December 1999.

Meanwhile, the larger Royal U.S. Index Fund (with $75 million in assets) escaped damage. It paid out 23 cents a unit in December 2000, up from 8 cents a year earlier.

Alan was shocked to find he had a taxable capital gain of $85,000 for 2000. Taken with his other income, that meant he would exceed the threshold for his OAS to be clawed back in full. He would also owe interest, since his quarterly income tax instalments were too low.

What made him feel worse: the capital gain was illusory. The fund actually lost money in 2000 as the U.S. market fell. But when he spoke up, Alan found the bank was willing to make him whole again.

A Royal Mutual Funds official said the fund tried to minimize taxable distributions, but couldn't avoid a large capital gains payout after the unexpected outflow of cash.

A small fund with few unitholders is vulnerable, he admitted. "But in any fund, cash flows through the year can trigger inadvertent capital gains."

If you own funds inside a registered plan, it's still important to be aware of annual distributions, because they can affect the price of a fund. You see this particularly with managers who are active traders.

Look at what happened in 1993 to Altamira Equity Fund. Manager Frank Mersch realized big capital gains by selling stocks at a profit during the year. In late December, Altamira Equity paid out a whopping capital gains dividend of $6.17. This pushed down the fund's net asset value to $28.14 from more than $34 before the payout.

The year-end surprise is less common with bond, mortgage and money market funds, since they make quarterly or monthly distributions. But with equity funds, if you buy in November or December, you may be taxed on someone else's income and pay more tax than you expected.

If you're a taxable investor, you should never buy a fund just before it distributes a substantial capital gain or income dividend. Wait till January to buy, if you can.

Also, ask the fund's sponsor about capital gains that have been realized but not distributed, as well as unrealized capital gains in the portfolio.

Wrap accounts can be costly

Mutual funds were supposed to simplify things for investors. But they've done the opposite. There are so many funds and so many choices that life has become even more confusing.

Pre-packaged portfolios can help make things simpler again. Also called "wraps," they consist of a half-dozen or so funds bundled together under one annual fee. Wraps appeal to investors who don't have the energy or expertise to manage their own portfolios.

Traditional wrap accounts offer a full range of securities for those with at least $50,000 to $100,000 to invest. They're a high-end product. But in the past few years, mutual fund managers have started offering wraps with much lower minimum investments.

Investors Group Inc., Canada's largest fund manager, has a number of pre-packaged portfolios. Mackenzie Financial Corp. offers two wrap programs; STAR uses only Mackenzie funds, while Keystone includes other funds. Banks are also active in the field, especially Bank of Montreal (MatchMaker), Toronto-Dominion (Managed Asset Program) and Royal Bank (Select Choices Portfolios).

Fees are all over the map. Some programs, such as Bank of Montreal's MatchMaker, have no extra cost beyond the annual management expense ratios of the funds. Mackenzie's STAR and Keystone programs charge a premium of one-tenth of a percentage point over the funds' management fees and expenses (with a minimum of $25 and a maximum of $100 a year). Opus 2 Direct.com sells fund portfolios over the Internet for an annual fee of 1.85 per cent (plus GST). That compares to a 2.99 per cent annual fee for the Artisan portfolios from Assante Financial Management Ltd.

Is a mutual fund wrap for you? It depends whether you're willing to pay more for convenience and one-stop shopping. Figure out if it's worth an extra cost (say $100 a year) to get a professionally diversified portfolio that is monitored regularly and rebalanced periodically.

If you have a good financial adviser, you may not need a wrap product—you're already getting that level of service. Do-it-yourself investors can find abundant advice on asset allocation (as well as model portfolios) in books, magazines and over the Internet.

Glorianne Stromberg, an investor advocate who has written several reports on mutual funds, questions the value of wrap programs. "All they do is add cost," she says. "If the extra money were compounding for you, you'd likely be more comfortable in your retirement. Why pay fees to fund someone else's retirement?"

Another problem is that performance can be hard to track. Wrap managers don't always publish results in newspapers. Those that publish results show performance that's no better or worse than stand-alone funds in their category.

Authors Gordon Pape, Richard Croft and Eric Kirzner analyzed the major packages (STAR, Keystone, Artisan, Investors Group, Spectrum and MatchMaker) and found no evidence they could outperform peer-group averages. "Based on what we've seen so far, the mutual fund packages have not been particularly impressive, although none has been absolutely awful, either," they said in *Investing Strategies 2001* (Prentice Hall Canada).

Surf your way to investment knowledge

What are the best Web sites for investors who want to know about stocks? Here's a guided tour with Mary Cordeiro, who worked at the Toronto-based resource centre, the Investor Learning Centre of Canada. (The ILC was set up in 1996 by the Canadian Securities Institute, the industry's national educational organization.) Cordeiro, an expert in helping people find answers, says the first thing you need is a good terminology guide. Since the lingo changes all the time, you'll find more current definitions online than in a dictionary.

Suppose you've seen references to a "poison pill," but you're not sure what this means. Turn on your Internet browser and go to www.investorwords.com. It defines poison pill as "any tactic by a company designed to avoid a hostile takeover. One example is the issuance of preferred stock that gives shareholders the right to redeem their shares at a premium after the takeover." As you read, you can click on an underlined term to get other definitions, like "hostile takeover" or "preferred stock."

Your next stop is www.investopedia.com, which has more Canadian content. Two young men in Edmonton, who call themselves the Investing Guys, give definitions and provide seamless links to Web sites such as The Motley Fool. If you want to know about growth stocks, Investopedia gives a definition—"shares in a company whose earnings are expected to grow at an above-average rate relative to the market"—and connects you to longer articles about growth investing.

Buzzwords are another thing Investopedia does well. What's a "macaroni defence"? It's when a company issues bonds that must be redeemed at a high price in a takeover—similar to a poison pill, but using bonds rather than equity.

The Investors Association of Canada has a glossary at its site, www.iac.ca, which includes home-grown terms like "GIC" and "strip bond." It's fairly short, however, and has nothing on, for example, EBITDA (earnings before interest, taxes, depreciation and amortization), a favourite accounting gimmick used to dress up a company's earnings.

Don't miss the Investor Learning Centre's Web site, www.investorlearning.ca. The frequently asked questions (FAQs), which number in the hundreds, are terrific. And there's always a topical question of the week, such as "What is a reverse stock split? Why might a company undergo such a split?"

After learning the language, you'll probably want to evaluate Canadian stocks and mutual funds. The place to go is SEDAR (the System for Electronic Document Analysis and Retrieval), www.sedar.com, which has public securities filings and company profiles. Suppose you're curious about Nortel Networks Corp. SEDAR has Nortel's quarterly results, news releases and reports of material change.

Before investing in a specific company, you need to look at prospects for the entire sector. The best place is Industry Canada's massive Strategis site, www.strategis.gc.ca. Go to Business Information by Sector, where you'll find a wealth of information about the companies in a sector (such as wineries) and the projected growth trends.

For sector analysis, there are two excellent books that must be mentioned. They're very expensive (about $100 apiece), but you can find them in reference libraries. *The Handbook of Canadian Security Analysis*, edited by Joe Kan (John Wiley & Sons), looks at the 14 industry sectors of the Toronto Stock Exchange 300 index. The first volume came out in 1997 and the second in 2000.

Finally, stock investors need to look at the competitive or external forces that will affect a company's performance. These include fiscal and monetary policies, exchange rates, money supplies, trade deficits, energy prices, inflation and global events.

For economic indicators, there are two Web sites you should bookmark: Statistics Canada (www.statcan.ca) and the Bank of Canada (www.bankofcanada.ca).

The major Canadian banks post economic data on their Web sites. You can get to them from the Canadian Bankers Association site (www.cba.ca). Click Links at the top of the home page.

There are many Internet portals for investors, but I'll mention just one I find handy. The Break Out Report (http://breakoutreport.com) leads you to dozens of other investment sites. Host Marco den Ouden, author of *The 50 Best Science and Technology Stocks for Canadians* (John Wiley & Sons) also runs portfolios and gives buy and sell recommendations.

part five

Financial Planning

Face it. You're never completely on your own when it comes to money. Every decision you make to spend, save or invest is made in the context of relationships to other people. Instead of personal finances, we should be talking about interpersonal finances.

Even when you're young and single with no dependents, you still have your parents to consider. You may want to start a savings plan to show them you're responsible with your money, or to pay them back for some of the help they've given you in the past. One day, you may be called upon to support your parents as they supported you.

Later when you marry, or get involved in a common-law union, you have to take your own and your partner's interests into account when making financial decisions. It's important to talk about money—or put your wishes into writing—before settling down with someone for a life-time together. But many couples don't like to broach the subject, fearing it may lead to disagreements.

If children come along, your expenses multiply. You start to save for their education and for any other special needs that arise (ortho-dontic work, piano lessons, snowboard equipment, summer camps—to name a few I've encountered with my kids). At the same time, you teach them to be responsible with their own money.

Once you become a parent, you think about things you may have ignored before. If you and your spouse die together in an accident, what happens to your children? Who gets your possessions? You realize it's time to write a will, so your survivors know what you want to happen after your death. And a power of attorney ensures that someone is there to make decisions at a time when you can't.

In your 40s and 50s, you may be part of the sandwich generation. While you're launching your kids into financial self-sufficiency, you're also helping your parents deal with new financial realities—retirement, illness, widowhood, moving from home to an institution or maybe coming to live with you. If they haven't gotten around to drafting a will or power of attorney, you tell them about how you've done yours and hope they take the hint.

In this final section, we'll look at your relationship to money and to the people in your life. We'll talk about how you can shift income from one family member to another. The Canadian tax system frowns on income splitting, but still offers a few ways to move money into the hands of those in a low tax bracket.

Then we'll look at different ways to save for post-secondary education. This advice applies not only to parents and grandparents but also to uncles and aunts and cousins and family friends. Education is the key to future success in the world. Don't be content with buying toys and clothes and compact discs for a child you love. Give a gift that lasts: Contribute to his or her college fund.

The next topic is financial planning for life's transitions—marriage, divorce and the death of a spouse. We'll look at the needs of unmarried couples, who don't get the same protection as married couples unless they sign a contract guaranteeing their rights to support after separation or death. We'll also give advice for same-sex relationships.

Finally, we'll address what happens when you die. Unpleasant as it may be to contemplate, death is inevitable and should be planned for in advance. Your family members deserve to be sheltered from the chaos that ensues when you haven't made any plans. They also need a document that designates someone to act on your behalf if you're incapacitated and can't act for yourself.

None of this is easy stuff to talk about or to put in writing. That's why most of us tend to wait till a crisis hits before dealing with the issues. But the need never goes away.

"No man is an island," said writer John Donne. We're entwined with others in families or romantic partnerships. This means we must think about their welfare, as well as our own, when making decisions and planning for the future. Money is always a shared concern.

Practise safe income splitting

Income splitting is a way to reduce taxes by taking money from higher-income family members and getting it into the hands of lower-income members. The savings can be substantial. That's because Canada has a progressive tax system. The higher your income, the higher a percentage of that income the tax collector is going to take.

Life would be simple if higher earners could simply hand over money to a spouse or children to be taxed at their rates. But there are special rules that catch people who try to do this.

The attribution rules found in Canadian tax law say that when you try to shift income to other family members with lower tax rates, you won't get away with it. The income will be shifted back to you and taxed in your hands.

Let's look at a single-income family in Ontario. Jim earns $60,000 at his full-time job, while Jane is a full-time homemaker. The family's tax bill last year was $14,349.

Living next door are Fred and Frieda, each earning $30,000 a year. Though the total income is the same as Jim and Jane's, this double-income family's tax bill is only $10,642. The tax saving of $3,707 a year is enough to send a child to university.

In Ontario, employment income up to $30,004 is taxed at the lowest rate (about 26 per cent). That's why Fred and Frieda pay less tax when each spouse earns $30,000.

But when Jim earns all the money himself, every dollar of income above $30,004 is taxed at about 39 per cent, giving rise to the family's higher tax bill. This happens no matter where you live in Canada: Single-income families generally pay more tax than double-income families. They're also penalized in retirement with higher taxes and pension clawbacks.

That's why it makes sense to transfer income among family members. Here are a few legal income-splitting tactics:

- If you have children under 18, give them cash to invest in a stock or mutual fund. The profit is taxable in their hands, not yours, when the investment is sold. Since the kids probably have no income, they won't pay tax on the gain. But any dividends or interest income earned on the gift will be attributed back to you.

- Instead of giving cash, you can transfer existing investments to the kids. This is considered a sale at fair market value, so you may have to pay tax if the assets you transfer have gone up in value. But that's small change compared to the taxes you'll save by putting the investments, and the future gains, in the kids' hands.

- Lend your children the money to buy an interest-bearing investment, such as a Canada Savings Bond or guaranteed investment certificate. You can't give children money to buy an interest-bearing investment or you will be trapped by the attribution rules. But if you lend money, the earnings will be taxed in the child's hands. This must be a real loan, with a commercial rate of interest and annual repayment terms.

Once children turn 18, you don't have to worry about gifts versus loans any more. The income generated on any investments you give will be taxed in their hands. It won't be attributed back to you, no matter what type of income it is.

The Canada Child Tax Benefit is also exempt from rules against income splitting. You can invest these monthly payments in the child's name and not pay tax on the investment earnings.

The Canada Child Tax Benefit, introduced in 1993, replaced the universal baby bonus. It's a more targeted payment that goes out to almost three million families. In order to get it, you have to file a tax return.

The basic benefit is $1,151 a year for each child under 18 (as of July 2002). For the third and each additional child, the benefit is $1,231 a year. There's an additional supplement of $228 a year for each child under seven years old when no child-care expenses are claimed. (The amounts are different in Alberta, where the government has decided to vary the basic benefit that residents receive.)

Once a family's income reaches $32,960 a year, the Canada Child Tax Benefit is reduced. But families with income of $79,000 a year still qualify for part of the basic benefit. This money is tax-free, and parents can invest the monthly payments in the child's name without worrying about the investment earnings being taxed back to them. The earnings are taxable in the child's hands, which means no tax is paid as long as his or her income is below the basic personal amount ($7,412 in 2002).

Even if you don't think you qualify for the child tax benefit, it's worth applying just in case. Fill out form RC66, Canada Child Tax Benefit Application, when your child is born or your adopted child comes to live with you. You should apply as soon as possible, because the government can make retroactive payments for up to only 11 months from the month it receives your application.

This is an income-tested benefit, which means both spouses or common-law partners must file tax returns on time each year. It's important to file a tax return even if you have no income to report.

The Canada Customs and Revenue Agency calculates the benefit based on information from your previous year's tax return. The size of your benefit depends on the net family income (what you earn after deductions such as RRSP contributions and child-care expenses).

To get the biggest child tax benefit possible, try to reduce your net income by maximizing RRSP contributions for both parents. If you separate from your spouse or partner, ask CCRA to base the benefits on the income of one spouse only. That should increase your payments.

If you put the child tax benefit into a registered education savings plan, you can collect the federal Canada Education Savings Grant of up to $400 a year. This is a great way to save for your child's education with capital provided entirely by the government.

Get Ottawa to subsidize your kids' education

The federal government will give you up to $7,200 to pay for a child's post-secondary education. It will top up your own savings with the Canada Education Savings Grant (CESG), launched in January 1998. This is free money, so why turn it down?

Post-secondary tuition costs are rising faster than inflation. Tuition went up 135 per cent in the decade of the 1990s, as governments cut back their funding.

The average arts and science undergraduate now pays $4,000. When all costs are considered—tuition, books, lodging and a computer—one year of study away from home in Canada starts at about $13,000.

Maybe your income will grow enough to fund the full cost of a child's post-secondary education. Or maybe your child will earn enough from part-time jobs to make a meaningful contribution. But who knows? It's better to get a head start by saving for education in a child's early years, as soon as he or she is born, and taking advantage of the government subsidy.

Here's how it works:

- Set up a registered education savings plan (RESP) with a bank, trust company, credit union, stockbroker, mutual fund manager or scholarship foundation. An RESP is a way of deferring taxes on your investment income until the child goes to college or university.

- Apply for a social insurance number for your child. You can do it as soon as the child is born. Ask your RESP provider for an application. A social insurance number is a legal requirement for the government grant. It's needed to ensure the program is run effectively and to maintain accurate records for each child.

- Contribute to the RESP. You can put in up to $4,000 a year or $42,000 over the life of the plan.

- The Canada Education Savings Grant adds 20 per cent to your first $2,000 in RESP contributions each year. The maximum CESG payment is $400 a year.

- You can carry forward the grant room to future years. Suppose you're short of cash and skip a year. If you contribute $4,000 the following year, you can get an $800 grant.

- RESP contributions are eligible for the government grant if they were made after Dec. 31, 1997, and before the end of the calendar year in which the child turns 17. There are special rules for children aged 16 or 17.

- You don't have to worry about applying for the grant each time you contribute to an RESP. The RESP trustee collects the money from the government on your behalf and adds it to your account.

The grant program is a big hit with parents and has doubled the number of RESP accounts in Canada. There are 1.8 million RESP accounts eligible for the grant, and Ottawa has paid almost $1 billion to RESP beneficiaries so far.

Still, overall awareness of the program is quite low. Government surveys show only 13 per cent of Canadians know about the grants and only 17 per cent know about RESPs. That's too bad, because even a modest amount of money can grow to a substantial nest egg if you start early and take advantage of the federal grants.

The government gives the example of Rick and Diane, who have a three-year-old named Hayley. If they put $25 every two weeks into Hayley's RESP, that adds up to $650 a year. Their investment will also earn a $130 Canada Education Savings Grant.

Over 15 years, Rick and Diane keep contributing at the same rate. They keep earning CESG money on top of their own savings. If all this money grows at five per cent a year, then Hayley will have almost $19,000 to help pay for her education.

Make sure the money is in the plan before Dec. 31 of each year. A timing error means you will lose up to $4,000 in RESP contribution room for the year. And that, in turn, means losing thousands of dollars in tax-deferred growth over the next 20 to 25 years.

Here's the story of one parent who missed the RESP deadline. In December 1998, Fred went to the bank to set up an RESP for his daughter, who had been born in October. He had $2,000 to invest.

Fred was anxious to receive the Canada Education Savings Grant, the government's way of rewarding those who put money aside for post-secondary education. Remember, with the CESG, you get a rebate of 20 per cent of your RESP contribution, up to a maximum of $400 in a calendar year.

Fred's newborn did not have a social insurance number, a prerequisite for the federal grant. He went ahead with the paperwork and gave the bank his daughter's SIN when it arrived in early 1999. He reported the SIN twice more to the bank before it was finally entered on September 28, 1999.

The delay meant the bank could not apply for the CESG until November 1999, and the grant wouldn't be paid until at least January 2000.

No problem, the bank said. It would backdate the $800 payment to when it should have arrived.

That wasn't the only problem. Fred's statement showed the RESP contribution was not deposited until January 1999.

No problem, the bank said. It would backdate the RESP contribution. Unfortunately for Fred, the bank goofed. Since his RESP deposit missed the December 31, 1998 deadline, it qualified as a 1999 contribution. It could not be backdated. As a result, he was able to add only $2,000 to the plan in 1999, not the $4,000 he wanted to contribute.

"With my daughter's birthday in October, as well as Christmas gifts, I'd intended to maximize the 1999 contribution," Fred told the bank. "With a 10 per cent annual return, the extra $2,000 investment would have grown to more than $20,000 over 25 years.

"I do not know of a comparable investment for my daughter, so this right provided by the federal government has been taken away."

Fred was even more annoyed to find that bank staff didn't fully understand the rules. The reason for the confusion: While you can carry forward unclaimed Canada Education Savings Grants, you cannot carry forward RESP contribution room.

It's easy to get confused, says chartered accountant Tim Cestnick in *Winning the Education Savings Game: RESPs and Other Strategies for Canadians* (Prentice Hall Canada).

CESG payments are governed by the Human Resources Development Act (HRDA), while RESPs are governed by the *Income Tax Act* (ITA). One act allows you to do things the other act won't allow you to do. "Yes, that's right, they sort of conflict with each other," Cestnick says.

Under the HRDA, your child is entitled to CESG room of $2,000 a year up to the year he or she turns 17. The HRDA also allows you to carry forward any unused CESG room. So if you don't make any RESP contributions for the next five years, your child will gain $10,000 of CESG room ($2,000 a year for five years).

You would think, then, that all you'd need to do in five years is to make a $10,000 contribution to your child's RESP. Then you'd receive a CESG payment of $2,000 (20 per cent of $10,000).

"In fact, there's nothing in the HRDA to stop you from doing this," says Cestnick. "Hold on, though. The ITA won't let you do it."

Under the *Income Tax Act*, the most you can contribute to an RESP in any year is $4,000. And if you fail to use that contribution room, you can't carry forward the $4,000 RESP limit for use in future years. The bottom line? You may never get to use up your CESG room if you don't make regular contributions to an RESP.

To find the cash for an RESP contribution, Cestnick provides a dandy tip: Use your RRSP refund for this purpose. A $5,000 contribution to a registered retirement savings plan will save you $2,000 in tax if you're the average Canadian. If you were to contribute that $2,000 refund to an RESP, your child would receive $400 in a Canada Education Savings Grant.

To return to our example above, Fred's bank did try to make amends for the RESP opportunity he lost in 1998 because of the processing delay. It promised a knapsack, then four movie tickets. "The offer was in no way intended to trivialize the extent of the problem or to minimize the frustration you have experienced," the bank said when Fred turned down both gifts as inadequate.

While still fighting over compensation, Fred wanted to get the message out about the December 31 deadline for RESP contributions. Parents should be aware, he says, that if a financial institution fails to meet the deadline, the government will not backdate and your contribution room will be forfeited.

A deadline provides a sense of urgency about contributing. But remember: You can be penalized for skating too close to the deadline. To be on the safe side, contribute early.

Questions to ask about RESPs

There are about 65 RESP providers who have signed an agreement with Human Resources Development Canada to receive grants on behalf of students. They're listed at HRDC's Web site (www.hrdc-drhc.gc.ca). This is helpful if you're shopping around, but you need to narrow down your search.

Start by deciding whether you want a self-directed or a group RESP. A self-directed RESP is more flexible. You control the types of investments, which can include mutual funds, stocks and bonds, and guaranteed investment certificates.

Group plans, also called scholarship trust plans, are less flexible. Your contributions are pooled with those of other subscribers and you have no say in how the money is invested. These plans are restricted to investing in government bonds, treasury bills, mortgage-backed securities or guaranteed deposits.

Equity investments carry a higher risk. Stock markets can plunge, taking your education savings along with them. If you choose a self-directed RESP, recognize that there are no safety nets. Your capital is at risk unless it's invested safely. You can play with hot stocks or funds in a child's babyhood, but you should move into lower-risk investments by the teenage years.

The second RESP decision you have to make is whether you want an individual or a family plan. An individual plan cannot have more than one beneficiary, while a family plan can. A family plan lets you allocate RESP income to any of the beneficiaries. So if one child doesn't go to college or university, the others can use the money for their post-secondary studies.

An individual plan lets you name anyone as a beneficiary. You can name yourself, your spouse, a niece or nephew or a family friend. But with a family plan, the beneficiaries must be connected to the subscriber by blood or adoption.

Flexibility is important because the RESP income must be used to pay for education. You don't want to forfeit some of the money if none of your children goes on to a post-secondary education after high school.

Flexibility of payouts is also a consideration. How much money can you take out of the RESP, and how quickly, once the child begins college or university studies?

The government places only one restriction on the timing of withdrawals, says Tim Cestnick in *Winning the Education Savings Game* (Prentice Hall Canada). During the first 13 weeks of an educational program, the total payments from an RESP cannot exceed $5,000. After 13 weeks, this restriction is gone.

The most flexible plans allow your child to make withdrawals from an RESP at any time, and even to withdraw all the funds in the first year. This isn't a great idea but it may be necessary.

Group plans usually require funds to be left in the RESP for withdrawal each year that the child is enrolled in an educational program. Parents may appreciate this inflexibility, since it ensures the money won't run out prematurely. But there's a risk of being short-changed if your child drops out after the first or second year.

When setting up an RESP, always ask about the fees. Group plans charge sales commissions based on the number of units you hold. You may get a refund of these up-front "membership fees" or "enrolment fees" if you remain in the plan until maturity. But if you collapse the plan early, the sales charges will be deducted from the refund.

Self-directed plans also have sales commissions, plus management fees and expenses if the money is in mutual funds. But the management fees are deducted every year, not up front.

With their front-loaded fees, group plans earn interest on the money for years. They can afford to refund your fees 18 years later and still come out ahead, even after paying commissions to the sales representatives.

The best option, of course, is not to quit the plan before it matures. If you're short of cash, ask the plan's sponsor if you can stop making payments for a while or reduce the number of units you hold.

Michael, a *Toronto Star* reader, found himself in financial difficulty after splitting up with his wife. He had invested almost $9,000 in an RESP, which he'd opened in 1995 when his daughter was two. Now he wanted to close the plan.

But when he called the RESP provider, USC Education Savings Plan, he was shocked to find the balance was only $6,460. The enrolment fees had cost him 28 per cent of the plan's value.

USC tried to keep his plan in force by offering to let him reduce his $125 a month payments and get fewer units. It also agreed to suspend his payments for up to two years, as long as he made up the difference later.

Michael didn't remember being told about the enrolment fees, though he had initialled a clause in the contract saying he was aware of them. All he remembered was feeling great pressure from the salesperson to sign up his two-year-old daughter right away.

Benjamin McLean, author of *Guarantee Your Child's Financial Future* (McGraw-Hill Ryerson), has listened to many sales presentations on RESPs. "You're given so much information that it doesn't take long before you are unable to retain what the costs are," he says. "And you feel unable to ask, because it's impolite."

It's important to realize that assets in RESPs have more than doubled to $7 billion as a result of the federal Canada Education Savings Grant. Banks, stockbrokers and mutual fund companies, which offer plans without high up-front fees, have $3.5 billion in assets or half of the market.

"When there was no competition, the pooled plans could get away with charging a front-end load. But it doesn't hold up any more," McLean says.

A USC official said the enrolment fees would be a bargain if Michael had stuck with the plan until his daughter was ready to go to university at age 18. Michael would have paid $24,233 into the plan and gotten back $21,631 in the first year (his original capital, minus $2,420 in enrolment fees and $182 in depository fees).

If his daughter had continued her post-secondary studies, Michael would have received RESP payments of $15,730 a year for the next three years—or $47,190 in total. (The estimate was based on what students in Michael's plan received in the years 1998 to 2000.)

But USC's projections did not impress Michael, who went ahead with his withdrawal of the money. He planned to start a new RESP at a bank. "The public needs to be informed," he says. "Before you jump into a plan, you need to know the fees involved."

Human Resources Development Canada, which administers the Canada Education Savings Grant, has a wealth of useful RESP information at its Web site. There are also links to providers' Web sites so you can compare plans.

I've heard many complaints about high-pressure selling by scholarship trust organizations over the years. And I, too, have sat through a few overzealous presentations. I signed up my two sons with the Canada Scholarship Trust Plan (and now gratefully receive RESP payments). But it took me a few years to get over my aversion to the canned sales pitches.

Customers should watch out for exaggerated claims. Salespeople often talk about the higher interest rates of a few years ago, without mentioning that the rates—and payouts to students—are lower now.

In June 2001, the six major scholarship trust organizations (known as the RESP Dealers of Canada) agreed to a voluntary code of sales practices. The code says salespeople should not be intrusive or tear down competitors. In addition, they shouldn't make any promises about an RESP's future value (because it depends on variables like future interest rates).

If you think an RESP representative has overstepped the bounds, call the company's head office. Then, if you're not satisfied, get in touch with the provincial securities commission. Salespeople have to pass a proficiency exam and take ongoing training to make sure their product knowledge and market awareness remain current.

Look at in-trust accounts for kids

RESPs have a reputation for being risky. That's because, in previous years, you could lose all the interest on your savings if your child's education ended with high school. The forfeited income would help other children enrolled in the plan to pursue post-secondary education, or it would be donated to an educational institution of your choice.

Thank goodness, the RESP rules were changed a few years ago to make the plans more flexible. If the original child decides not to pursue a post-secondary education, you can substitute another child in the family. You can even name yourself or your spouse as an RESP beneficiary, as long as you're willing to give up your job and go back to school full-time.

It's now easier to get access to RESP funds not used for education. You can withdraw the money in the plan (contributions and income) and pay tax at your regular rate, plus a 20 per cent penalty. Or you can transfer up to $50,000 from an RESP to your registered retirement savings plan, if you have enough RRSP contribution room.

In both cases, the RESP must have been in existence for at least 10 years. And all the beneficiaries must be age 21 or over and ineligible to receive educational assistance payments from the plan.

Given these withdrawal options, tax expert Tim Cestnick says parents should take care when setting up an RESP. Consider naming both yourself and your spouse as joint subscribers of the plan. Then, if it's necessary to roll RESP assets into an RRSP later, you'll have the choice of which spouse's RRSP to use.

"If the grandparents are subscribers, there's a good chance they will no longer have an RRSP, since they could be over age 69," Cestnick advises in *Winning the Education Savings Game.*

"Thought should be given, then, to making the parents the subscribers of the plan, even if this means that the grandparents give their contributions to the parents, who then contribute it to the RESP."

Even with the greater flexibility, RESPs still carry some risk. The future is uncertain and you can't predict what newborns will do when they grow up. What if they never get to the post-secondary level or drop out of programs they agreed to take? You may find the option of moving money to your RRSP doesn't work because you don't have enough contribution room.

You may also find the RESP limits too low, especially if you luck into an inheritance or work-related bonus. You can put in only $4,000 a year for each beneficiary, with a lifetime maximum of $42,000.

With an in-trust account, another popular way of saving for education, there are no limits on how much you can invest each year.

Mutual fund companies, banks, trust companies, credit unions and investment dealers can set up in-trust accounts for children under 18. The goal is income splitting, as explained earlier, since capital gains earned on the investments will be taxed in the child's hands.

But there's one big danger with an in-trust account. Children can use the assets for any purpose—buying a car, taking a trip or launching a business—once they turn 18.

Even as a donor, you have no right to say how the funds are used. Nor can you insist the money be spent on education, or spread out over the three or four years of a degree program. That stops a lot of parents cold when they consider the implications. "A rebellious teen with thousands of dollars suddenly at his disposal is not a pleasant thought to contemplate," say Gordon Pape and Frank Jones in *Head Start: How to Save for Your Children's or Grandchildren's Education* (Stoddart).

As an alternative, you can set up a formal trust, also called a family trust or "inter vivos trust." You would attach conditions to the trust to prevent your child from squandering the money later on.

Setting up such a trust will cost you $1,000 or more initially. There will be annual trustee fees, usually based on a percentage of assets in the account, and annual tax returns will have to be filed.

"The bottom line is that, in practical terms, this option is really available only to the well-off," say Pape and Jones.

But a formal trust has an advantage over an in-trust account, since it continues beyond the child's eighteenth birthday. You don't have to hand over the assets at the age of majority.

Any trust, whether formal or informal, requires three participants: the beneficiary, who receives the money; the donor, who puts up the money; and the trustee, who manages the assets. The donor and the trustee must not be the same person. Otherwise, the trust may be voided and the income-splitting benefits lost.

When parents set up an in-trust account, one of them should take on the role of donor while the other acts as the trustee.

It's a good idea for the trustee to sell profitable investments and reinvest the money every few years. This increases the adjusted cost base of the investments, which means lower taxable gains later.

Don't even consider transferring money from an in-trust account to an RESP. That's because there are different rules for how contributors can recover their capital.

With an RESP, you can take back your contributions at any time without paying tax. (That's because the money you contribute to an RESP has already been taxed.) But with an in-trust account, you have no right to take back the assets: They belong to the child.

An in-trust account is, therefore, a safer haven for a child's education savings. The assets can't be liquidated and spent for other purposes when spouses split up. The money must stay invested on the child's behalf until he or she turns 18.

Life insurance can be used for education

Buying life insurance for your child can be a way to save for his or her post-secondary education. Life insurance offers a tax deferral similar to what's available with a registered education savings plan or an in-trust account.

I'm not talking about term insurance, which pays off only in the event of a death. I'm talking about cash value policies, which combine life insurance on a child with a savings or investment component. Part of the premium pays for insurance and the other part is invested for the child.

With cash value insurance, the savings or investment component grows tax-free for years and is taxed only when withdrawn. Since post-secondary students have little other income, the tax payable should be non-existent or very low.

If your aim is simply to accumulate cash for education, the RESP is a better choice. That's because you get a 20 per cent grant on top of your contributions from the federal government. Life insurance policies are not registered as RESPs, so you can forget about the grant.

Remember, too, you'll be giving up some of your education savings to buy life insurance for the child. Why do kids need insurance?

They have no dependents to provide for and no income to replace.

Sellers use a medical argument. They advise you to insure children when they're young and healthy, rather than wait till they're adults and possibly uninsurable.

At the age of majority, the child uses the investment income to pay for post-secondary studies. Meanwhile, the life insurance coverage stays in place and provides cheap ongoing protection.

Unlike an RESP, a life insurance policy has no contribution limit and no restrictions on how the money is used. So if the child does not go beyond high school, the extra savings in a policy may be withdrawn for other purposes. Sometimes you have to borrow against the cash value to get the money out.

An advantage of life insurance over an in-trust account is there's no age at which control of the plan's assets must be transferred automatically from parent to child.

"If the 18-year-old turns out to be a rebellious ingrate who has no intention of going to college," say Pape and Jones in *Head Start*, "the parent can retain control of the invested money indefinitely in hopes time will mellow the child or at least instil some degree of responsibility."

Universal life can be a good product for those who choose the insurance route. Most policies offer a wide choice of guaranteed and fixed-income investments, as well as index-linked deposits if you want some equity exposure.

Agents often produce an attractive projection of how your money will grow. Make sure they use realistic interest rates and stock market returns. Ask how long the interest rate is guaranteed.

Other questions: What is the true return after deducting the pure insurance cost? Will the insurance cost rise each year or every few years? What portion of the withdrawal will be taxable? What are the cancellation fees?

Search for scholarships and bursaries

Planning ahead is great, but not everyone manages to do it. Bursaries, grants and scholarships help close the financing gap when you haven't saved enough for a child's higher education.

You can find thousands of dollars in free money for students on the Internet. Two Web sites in particular are worth investigating: www.studentawards.com and www.scholarshipscanada.com.

Once you complete a profile outlining your child's interests and fields of study, these Web sites search for matching awards. You then choose which ones to apply for. The service is free. The average student qualifies for 15 scholarships, says Joe Freedman, who started Studentawards.com in 1998. The site has 350,000 registered users.

"A lot of private award administrators, such as corporations and not-for-profit groups, are finding us," he says. "They had no vehicle for getting these awards out to the public before."

The Canada Millennium Scholarship Foundation, established by the federal government in 1998, provides bursaries to students of merit who are in financial need. Students must have successfully completed a year of post-secondary studies. For details on applying, check out www.millenniumscholarships.ca.

The average bursary from the Millennium Scholarship Foundation is $3,000. However, students who get this money may have their provincial loans reduced by the same amount. Make sure to find out what the student loan rules are in your province.

Another Web site to check out is www.debtfreegrad.com. Murray Baker of Vancouver, author of a financial survival guide for students, *The Debt-Free Graduate* (HarperCollins), provides many useful tips and strategies. He has a calculator that lets students figure out what resources they have and what they need, and he publishes an online magazine, *The Money-Runner*.

Finally, you can't ignore the government's interactive Web site, www.canlearn.ca. It's a one-stop resource to help you decide what and where to study and how to cover the costs. CanLearn is an initiative of the student loans program directorate of Human Resources Development Canada, with the participation of all provinces and territories and over 25 Canadian learning and career development organizations.

Think of marriage as a business partnership

Here's a tip for any couple planning to get married: Prepare a list of everything you own and everything you owe before the wedding.

Marriage is a romantic partnership, but it's also a business partnership. Your assets will be commingled and divided equally in the event of divorce or death.

Nancy Bullis, a lawyer in Toronto, gives the example of a woman whose husband left her after seven years of marriage. She came into the marriage with a home the couple lived in throughout the years they were together.

Her friends told her to get a contract to exclude the home. She wouldn't listen. Nor did she bother to get the home assessed as of the wedding date. Now she'd have to share the proceeds from the sale with her former husband.

Another woman entered into marriage with a large inheritance from her aunt. She used the money to buy a family cottage. When she divorced her husband, she found she had unwittingly put her entire inheritance into an asset that was subject to equalization under Ontario family law. She could have used that money to help rebuild her life.

"But I don't have a home or an inheritance," you say. "Why do I need to add up what I own when I get married?"

You may have other valuable assets—a pension plan from your employer, money in a bank account, cars, jewelry, antiques, china, silver or computers.

Once you have an up-to-date list of what you own, you're better prepared to protect any worth you bring into the marriage if the relationship doesn't work out.

"Think of it as insurance," Bullis says in her book, *To Have and to Hold: The Smart Woman's Guide to Money and Marriage* (McGraw-Hill Ryerson), co-authored with Kathleen Aldridge. "Insurance is a smart move, not a pessimistic one. Having your finances in order and properly documented before you marry is smart."

As well as listing assets, you need to know what debts you and your partner are bringing into the marriage. You'll be sharing liabilities, too, once your finances are united.

You can go a step further by getting a marriage contract. This is a document that puts your wishes on paper with respect to property division, support and children. Some of these matters that fall under provincial legislation can be waived with a marriage contract. Some cannot. Make sure you get good legal advice.

Not everyone likes the idea of full disclosure of assets and debts. It may show up embarrassing inequalities between the partners. Still, you set a pattern by discussing finances openly at the beginning of a marriage. It can become a natural part of your lives together.

Bullis suggests couples continue to talk about money in a serious way. Once a year, perhaps on their wedding anniversary, they should set aside time to do a family annual report. This would involve looking at what you've done during the year to reduce debts, pay off your mortgage, save for retirement and increase your net worth.

Understand obligations of common-law partners

Once it was considered a sin to live together as man and wife without a marriage certificate. Today, 15 per cent of Canadian couples are in a common-law relationship. And eight per cent of children live with common-law parents. It's important for common-law partners to understand their obligations to each other if they split up.

British Columbia was the first province to require financial support between common-law spouses who had been living together for at least two years. Now most provinces give a common-law partner the right to claim financial support, as long as an application to court is made within a year of separation.

Every province defines things differently. In Ontario, couples qualify as spouses for support purposes if they have lived together for three years. If they have a child together, they will be treated as spouses, no matter how long they've cohabited.

Nova Scotia enforces support if the couple has been together one year, while Manitoba requires a couple to live together for five years if there are no children. New Brunswick specifies a "natural" child; other provinces include adopted children.

If you separate, you have the right to claim support on the basis of need and the other person's ability to pay. Support is calculated in exactly the same way as if you were married.

But common-law partners, unlike married spouses, don't have the right to share property acquired while they lived together. Property in a partner's name will continue to belong to him or her, unless the other partner has made a contribution to the property.

Common-law spouses who want to claim property from the other partner after separating have an expensive legal fight ahead of them, says Toronto lawyer Michael Cochrane. They have to prove they are entitled to anything at all. The same is true in death. A common-law spouse is not automatically entitled to a share of the deceased spouse's estate, unless he or she has been provided for in a will. If there's no will, there's no inheritance. Family members, such as legally married spouses and children, have priority claims.

Government pension plans are an exception. Most recognize a common-law spouse's right to claim a pension after the partner's death. Some private pension plans also consider people who cohabit to be legally married for the purpose of receiving a pension. However, employers are free to define how many years of living together are required.

The Canada Pension Plan considers a common-law partner a surviving spouse if the couple was living together in a conjugal relationship at the time of death and for a continuous period of at least one year. It also gives common-law spouses the right to an equal division of CPP pension credits after separation, if they have lived together for at least one year.

A cohabitation contract complements a will and protects couples living together outside marriage. It sets out the rights and duties within the relationship and in the event of a separation or death.

Cohabitation agreements are valid in Ontario, Quebec, New Brunswick, Prince Edward Island, Newfoundland, British Columbia and the territories. It's important for each party to get independent legal advice to make sure the contract can be enforced.

When it comes to income tax, you're considered to be common-law if you have lived with your partner for at least a year or if you have a child together. This has been the case since 1993. The federal government allows common-law spouses to use common income-splitting tactics, such as contributing to spousal RRSPs and pooling charitable donations and medical expenses.

Being considered married for tax purposes has a downside, too. Both spouses cannot claim the principal residence exemption, and the lower-income partner must claim child-care expenses. (This could mean reduced tax savings.) Total family income is used to determine eligibility for the child tax benefit, GST tax credit and provincial tax credits.

New rights for same-sex partners

Homosexual acts were once considered criminal offences in Canada. Prime Minister Pierre Trudeau, who said, "The state has no business in the bedrooms of the nation," amended the law in 1969.

Even in the 1970s and 1980s, same-sex partners had few legal rights and continued to be discriminated against when it came to jobs, housing and immigration. But the 1990s saw a significant expansion of same-sex legal rights. Members of the gay and lesbian community successfully pressed claims for equal treatment through the courts and human rights tribunals, using the equality provisions of the *Charter of Rights and Freedoms*.

In 1999, the federal government introduced an omnibus bill to extend to same-sex couples who have lived together for a year the same rights and responsibilities given to common-law opposite-sex couples. The bill covers income taxes, Old Age Security, the Canada Pension Plan and registered retirement savings plans, allowing same-sex partners to contribute to spousal RRSPs and get tax-free rollovers on death. The omnibus bill became law in June 2000. For the first time, the Canada Customs and Revenue Agency required all same-sex couples to declare their status on the 2001 tax return.

Canada has a self-assessment system, but the tax department points out that those who don't tell the truth can be penalized by reassessment of past returns and loss of income-based benefits. "Besides, clients who fail to identify themselves as common-law partners in order to avoid losing some benefits may well find that they are also depriving themselves of important fiscal advantages and pension rights as well," says a CCRA fact sheet.

While Ottawa has given rights to same-sex couples, provincial governments have not allowed them to legally marry. However, that may change in future because of a recent Supreme Court decision upholding same-sex marriages.

Same-sex couples have no right to property division and support if they separate. They also have no right to inherit property if one partner dies without a will. Even the rules for common-law cohabitation agreements don't apply to same-sex couples. That's why same-sex couples should write domestic contracts to help with their personal affairs.

"How can same-sex couples be sure that a court will be disposed to hold their cohabitation agreements valid and enforceable?" asks lawyer Michael Cochrane in his book, *For Better or for Worse: The Canadian Guide to Marriage Contracts and Cohabitation Agreements* (John Wiley & Sons).

"Well, for one thing, they could follow the law exactly as it has been designed to deal with the relationships they most resemble— common-law couples. Such an approach makes it very easy for a court to support their goals as expressed in the agreement."

Cohabitation agreements are not widely used, even among heterosexual couples. Cochrane estimates that fewer than five per cent of all unmarried couples have one.

A cohabitation agreement is a financial planning device that's especially important for same-sex couples, since they can't fall back on the various family law and divorce acts. "In same-sex couples, there should be a race to bring the subject up. Don't be shy," he says. Couples are strengthening their relationship with a cohabitation agreement, regardless of how much or how little protection they incorporate in it.

How to share assets after divorce

Married couples once had to prove adultery, cruelty, desertion or other misconduct to get a divorce. In 1968, the law was changed to allow couples to divorce after a separation of three years. And since 1986, couples can get divorced after one year's separation.

About 69,000 couples split up in 1998, according to Statistics Canada, down from a record 81,000 in 1989. Based on that rate, 36 per cent of marriages are expected to end in divorce.

Couples are marrying and divorcing later in life. The marriages that end in divorce last an average 13.7 years. Men are on average 42 years old when they divorce, while women are 40 years old.

Only in 1978 were the first laws passed requiring husband and wife to share some assets when a marriage broke down. Today, there must be an almost equal sharing of all the family's assets, including investments, pensions and businesses.

Since the 1990s, courts have been more generous in awarding spousal and child support, says Toronto lawyer Linda Silver Dranoff in *Everyone's Guide to the Law* (HarperCollins).

Even with rising support payments, Statistics Canada reported in 1997 that women and children who received support showed a 33 per cent decline in their standard of living one year after the separation. In contrast, men paying support had a 20 to 25 per cent improvement in their financial situation.

"It is wise for spouses to think through the consequences of marital separation and plan for it beforehand," advises Dranoff, a family lawyer in private practice for 27 years and a legal columnist with *Chatelaine* magazine.

Custody of the children and possession of the family home are priority issues. If the parents can't agree, they should remain in the home with the children until the decisions have been made and the financial arrangements nailed down.

If you're having marital problems and considering separation, you should put money aside in advance, Dranoff suggests. Also, be cautious when entering into new financial arrangements with a spouse. This is not the time to co-sign a loan or remortgage the house to raise money for a spouse's business or pay off your spouse's debts.

However, this is the time to start gathering information about the value of your assets and debts. Eventually, if you get a divorce, you have to complete a financial statement provided by your lawyer to help figure out the family's spending patterns now and in the future.

"If you can't complete this properly—if you don't know what you're paying for taxes, entertainment, vacations, food, rent and medical expenses—you won't be able to paint a clear enough picture for the judge," says financial author Gail Vaz-Oxlade in *A Woman Of Independent Means* (Stoddart).

"Remember, your financial statement is considered evidence under the rules of the court; so if you don't give complete evidence, the judge has less to work with, and that might be reflected in his or her decision."

Women whose spouses haven't shared information with them should scour the house for tax returns, investment information, insurance details, everything that might be pertinent to the settlement. "It's time to become informed," Vaz-Oxlade urges women. "You must rectify your lack of knowledge to protect yourself, and perhaps your children."

Financial statements are intended to save time and money by ensuring complete disclosure early in the legal process. Your credibility is at risk if the financial statement is not honestly completed and kept up to date throughout the proceedings, says lawyer Michael Cochrane in *Surviving Your Divorce* (John Wiley & Sons). It may be necessary, from time to time, to file amended financial statements showing updates and corrections.

Until 1978, spouses had no right to claim a share of any property accumulated by the other spouse during their marriage. But today, every province in Canada requires spouses to share assets when a marriage breaks down.

The rules on property division are complex. "It is not possible to say simplistically that everything is 50/50," says Toronto lawyer Linda Silver Dranoff. "In fact, not all assets are shared in every jurisdiction; nor is every asset split equally."

Most provinces provide time limits for a spouse to claim a share of the property in the other spouse's name. It must be done within a certain period after the marriage breaks down and the spouses separate. For this reason, it's important for both spouses to agree on a date of separation. This is also the date in many provinces on which the assets to be shared are valued.

Dranoff says the laws in Alberta, Saskatchewan, Manitoba, Ontario, Prince Edward Island, the Northwest Territories and Nunavut allow for the most extensive sharing of assets on separation.

The matrimonial home is a special case, since it's often the couple's main asset. In Ontario, British Columbia, New Brunswick, Newfoundland, Nova Scotia, Saskatchewan and Yukon, the entire value of the home is shared—even if one spouse owned it and brought it into the marriage. The only expectation is when a spouse brings a home into the marriage and has it exempted in a prenuptial agreement.

When the marriage ends, either or both spouses can apply to the court for an order giving one of them exclusive possession of the matrimonial home. The right of a spouse to live in the matrimonial home on separation cannot be waived by signing a marriage contract.

If a spouse puts an inheritance into the home (to renovate or pay down the mortgage) in British Columbia, Manitoba, Newfoundland, Ontario or Saskatchewan, the value of the home will still be shared.

Pensions are an asset that must be divided, but they're not easy to value. "You should be aware that those who do pension valuations do not work for free," says lawyer Michael Cochrane in *Surviving Your Divorce* (John Wiley & Sons). "Their bills for valuation can represent a significant disbursement on your lawyer's account, a disbursement that is eventually passed on to you."

Canada Pension Plan credits must also be shared when a marriage breaks down. This benefits a spouse who didn't work outside the home and wasn't eligible to make CPP contributions. But the pension credits would be relatively unchanged if both spouses had relatively equal incomes throughout the marriage.

Spouses who wish to divide their RRSP holdings evenly can "roll over" funds from one to the other without paying tax at the time of transfer. They must sign forms approved by the tax department, says Dranoff. If a person simply cashes some of his or her RRSP holdings in order to pay an equalizing amount to the other, tax would be payable. In any event, the recipient will pay tax when the RRSPs are eventually cashed in.

Women who have stayed out of the work force to raise a family or who have lower-paying jobs should hold onto RRSP assets—especially if the spouse has a company pension plan to rely on.

"Often, women choose to keep the family home, giving up retirement assets in exchange," says author Gail Vaz-Oxlade. "But this isn't always a smart move. With expensive upkeep and slow increases in real estate values, a home can become an albatross, inhibiting women from building the investment reserves they need to take care of themselves in later years."

You'll be starting from ground zero if you relinquish RRSP assets totally, Vaz-Oxlade advises stay-at-home wives in their late 40s or 50s. They have less time to build a strong retirement-asset base.

Ending fights about child support

Divorcing couples used to fight about child support, since there were no rules about how much a parent who paid child support should contribute. These fights became far less frequent when new guidelines on child support came into effect May 1, 1997.

The federal government devised a system for calculating an appropriate amount of child support. It takes into account the paying parent's annual income, the province or territory of residence and the number of children eligible for support. As a result, parents can agree on child-support amounts without going to court. And if they ask the court to decide on child support, the judge must refer to the guidelines in setting the amount.

The federal government's Web site, http://canada.justice.gc.ca, has an eight-step formula that lets parents estimate how much child support would be appropriate in their own case. You can also get a copy by calling 1-888-373-2222.

Consider, for example, a father of two children under 19 living in Ontario, who has an annual income of $75,000. His ex-wife has sole custody of the children, meaning they live with her at least 60 per cent of the time.

The table shows the father would be required to pay $979 a month in child support for the two children. If he had only one child, he would pay $605. If he had three kids, he'd pay $1,279. And if he had four, he'd pay $1,523.

The courts may order a higher amount if there are special or extraordinary expenses, or if the paying parent has an income of more than $150,000 a year. They may reduce the amount if there is shared or split custody, or if using the guidelines causes undue hardship.

The guidelines do not automatically change existing child-support orders or agreements, unless one of the parents wants to change the amount and gets a new court order.

The tax treatment of child support was also revised in 1997. No longer do receiving parents include child-support payments as income, nor do paying parents claim child support payments as a deduction. However these changes don't automatically apply to child-support orders and agreements made before May 1, 1997.

There are no federal guidelines when it comes to spousal support. Obviously, the size of the child support payment may affect the amount of spousal support. The courts usually keep an eye on both requirements when making support awards in these cases.

Spousal-support payments are treated differently from child support for tax purposes. Spousal support must be included in the recipient's income if it's paid periodically under a court order or written agreement. It's deductible from the income of the payer.

Those who need more information about family law and finances can refer to a wonderfully rich Web site, www.familylawcentre.com. Set up and maintained by family lawyer Joel Miller of Ricketts Harris in Toronto, the Web site also lists lawyers across Canada who practise family law.

Preserving financial
health for widows

Older women can expect to spend many years on their own after their spouse has died. Of almost 1.5 million people in Canada who have lost their spouse, widows outnumber widowers by five to one. According to Statistics Canada, eight per cent of women are widowed.

Today's widows are healthier, more active and living longer than any previous generation of women in human history. But longer life spans increase the risk that these women will outlive their retirement savings. "For many, their most limiting health problem may turn out to be their financial health," says Benjamin McLean, author of *The Canadian Widow's Guide* (McGraw-Hill Ryerson).

This generation of women has been paid less, contributed less to government and company pensions and spent more time out of the work force than men. "Many women are distressed to learn too late that their conservative personal savings accounts and term deposits, after years of service fees and inflation, have left them with inadequate buying power to meet their needs," McLean says.

Widows need good financial advice to help make their savings last. Should they inherit a husband's advisers or look for new ones? The greater the assets in a household, the more likely it was that the husband made all the financial decisions. But his investment personality and advisers may not suit the wife left behind.

Many widows have never managed money before. Some have never even written a cheque. "Widows are generally scared to death," says Betty Jane Wylie, who lost her husband at a young age and whose book, *Beginnings: A Book for Widows* (available on Amazon.com), is a classic in the field.

Benjamin McLean, who runs his own financial marketing company in Toronto, is a member of a church. A widow there asked him to recommend a book that would help her manage her retirement savings. When he couldn't find such a book, he decided to write one.

His last chapter, "Tips from the Merry Widows" (a support group at the church), on staying solvent, active and healthy, is a delight. "Don't throw in the trowel," for example, notes that women over 50 who garden once a week have higher bone density readings than those who jog, swim or do aerobics.

When it comes to financial advisers, here's McLean's list of questions to ask:

- Are they sensitive to your grief?

- Do they take the time to explain what is being done?

- Do they encourage you to bring a trusted friend or family member to the meetings?

- Are you confident in taking the advice you've been offered so far?

If you can't honestly answer yes, you should be looking for a new adviser, he tells widows. When firing your husband's adviser, do it with care and courtesy, by phone or in writing. Let the adviser know you've appointed someone else, appropriate to the financial plan you want to pursue.

"Use the opportunity to thank them once more," McLean says. "You never know when you might need their help again."

Dealing with a
terminal illness

Bonney, 54, was diagnosed with breast cancer five years ago. She knows her illness is terminal but, depending on how fast the cancer spreads, she might live for six months or for another two or three years.

The uncertainty makes it hard to plan for the future. But she has some big decisions to make. Should she continue living on long-term disability insurance? Or retire and take a pension now? What to do with the profit from selling her house and downsizing to an apartment? How to minimize taxes on the estate she will leave to her two adult sons?

"I want to get my financial affairs in order," Bonney told me. But she's been busy with medical treatments and hasn't had time to get professional advice.

Money is tight, as well. Her income of $37,000 a year barely covers living expenses in downtown Toronto, not to mention health-related costs not paid for by private insurance or medicare.

Financial planner Warren Baldwin agreed to waive his fees to help Bonney and others in a similar position. His key message: Don't wait till critical illness strikes to get your financial life in shape.

Suppose you go to the doctor and find you have a condition serious enough to require surgery the same day. You'll probably be in hospital for a few weeks, using all your energy to recuperate. You won't have time to get your will up to date, your papers organized, your insurance in place. So why not do it now?

Bonney has always paid attention to her personal finances. As a language teacher with the Toronto District School Board, she brought up two children on her own. She also got a real estate licence and sold houses in her spare time, hoping to leave teaching one day.

When she became ill in October 1996, she was earning $65,000 a year as an elementary school teacher. She needed aggressive treatment and hasn't been able to work since. When we spoke, she was on permanent chemotherapy, with two weeks on and one week off.

She rented a co-op apartment on Toronto's waterfront after selling her east-end home. "I couldn't afford it or maintain it," she says. "I was just getting further into debt."

When she and I talked, the $15,000 profit she made on her house was in a low-interest savings account at the bank. She wanted the money to be accessible, in case she has the strength to go away on trips. "Travel and genealogy are my passions," she says.

Bonney's income breaks down as follows: just under $27,000 a year tax-free from a long-term disability plan sponsored by her employer; $10,000 in taxable disability payments from the Canada Pension Plan; and a few hundred dollars in interest.

Once she adds in all her expenses, there's not much left over. She pays $949 a month for rent, $154 a month for health insurance, $160 monthly for household help, $130 a month to rent a machine that delivers electric-impulse therapy for pain relief, $300 monthly for lymphatic drainage massages and $40 per month for hospital parking.

Baldwin spent six hours with Bonney, assessing her financial situation and giving written recommendations.

On her first question—"Do I continue living on disability insurance, or retire and take a pension now?"—his answer was clear: Don't retire from teaching.

Retirement means losing her life insurance, which is for only active employees. It's a benefit worth $80,000 to her survivors when she dies. Furthermore, she would earn less from her pension (which is taxable) than from long-term disability (which is not taxable). Her after-tax pension income would be $14,943 a year. Long-term disability pays her $26,783 a year, a net improvement of $12,000, or 80 per cent more than the pension.

On her second question—"Where do I invest the $15,000 profit from selling my house?"—Baldwin suggested opening an account with a bank that pays high interest rates of two to three per cent on every dollar of savings. Virtual banks, such as ING Direct or President's Choice Financial, make sense for someone like Bonney, "who's quite computer-literate and not mobile," says Baldwin. "She would have point-and-click access to her money at all hours of the day or night."

Bonney was hoping to give her $15,000 savings to her son Bruce to help him buy a house, but Baldwin nixed the idea. "This would leave you short of liquid assets when you might need them most," he said. Could Bruce, burdened with a large mortgage, repay the money at the drop of a hat? What if there were a new cancer treatment or medication she had to subsidize?

As Baldwin says, "She can write a cheque to her son, but there's quite a risk. Consider that money gone."

On the third question—"How can I minimize the taxes on my estate?"—Baldwin suggested she designate her sons as beneficiaries of her life insurance, pension and registered retirement savings plan. This would ensure the assets would pass to them directly, without going through her will and attracting probate taxes.

Bonney could also register her bank accounts and high-interest savings accounts in joint name with her sons. The downside: She could lose her financial independence.

Baldwin's final suggestion was to write off medical expenses, which would give Bonney a 25 per cent rebate. She hadn't used the tax break for medical expenses, since she had little taxable income. The solution? Take money out of her RRSP each year and claim medical expenses against it. If she does things right (by taking out enough money from her RRSP to write off her medical expenses), the effect will be that she pays no tax on the withdrawals.

Bonney was grateful for the advice, which Baldwin delivered in a way she found compelling and simple. While disappointed that she couldn't help her son buy a house, she knew she had to hold onto her savings.

"I don't know if I have six months or two to three years," she said. "That's what makes planning so difficult."

Once you're sick, you may be confronted with tough financial decisions you can't handle on your own and, at the same time, you'll be fending off well-meaning comments from friends and neighbours. "Free advice can be worth less than what you paid for it," Baldwin says. "Would you trust a medical opinion given over the backyard fence?"

Write a will for family harmony

If you're an adult, you need a will. It doesn't matter how much money you have or how many loved ones you leave behind.

A will ensures your property will go to the people you want to receive it. It allows you to make provisions for young children and create trusts for their benefit.

You can name an executor, someone to take care of distributing your assets when you're no longer around. If you die without a will, the government distributes your assets according to the laws of the province. This may produce results you don't want.

Without a will, you may not be able to help out elderly parents or leave gifts for nieces and nephews, friends and charities. And your children will inherit everything when they turn 18. That's a young age to burden kids with financial responsibility.

But surveys show only half of Canadians have an up-to-date will. It's not an affordability issue. You can prepare a will without a lawyer for about $30 using a do-it-yourself will kit.

I think the reason is that it's unpleasant to entertain thoughts about your own death. Not only do you have to make tough decisions about disposing of your property, but you also have to pick someone to administer your estate and look after any young children.

Then, once you make these decisions, you're supposed to tell the people you've designated as executors and guardians. That can be a difficult conversation.

I speak from experience. My husband and I first thought about drafting wills when we became parents, but kept dragging our feet. Should we choose his sister or my brother as our kids' guardian? Neither of us wanted to slight the other's family. We finally went with my brother, who was younger. When we got up the nerve to tell him, he said he'd chosen us as guardian for his kids, too. But he hadn't gotten around to telling us yet. All this procrastination meant we didn't finish our wills until our older son was 12 and the younger was seven. It's a good thing their parents weren't wiped out in a plane crash, leaving them as orphans!

We decided not to use a homemade will. Instead, we found a lawyer who specialized in estate planning and knew how to take the angst out of the proceedings. She also made sure all the i's were dotted and t's were crossed. Do-it-yourself wills can be problematic, says Toronto lawyer Margaret Rintoul, who heads the Canadian Bar Association's estate planning division. They're designed to cover common situations, such as married couples who want to leave everything to the surviving spouse and then divide assets equally with the children. This may not fit your own family.

"If you buy a kit, you must have the discipline to do it and finish it," says Rintoul. "These are emotional decisions and the fact you're doing your will at home rather than at a lawyer's office won't make them any easier."

Many people using will kits make mistakes, such as not signing or witnessing the wills properly. There's a requirement to have two witnesses, who are not beneficiaries or the spouse of a beneficiary.

"Do-it-yourself wills can be dangerous to your wealth," says Toronto estate lawyer Edward Olkovich. "After you've gone, your loved ones may live to regret it. Like most quick fixes, they can end up costing a lot more time and money. Worse still, a court can declare these wills invalid." What can go wrong with a will kit?

Olkovich thinks the main risk is improper drafting, which can lead to family feuds, estate delays and extra legal costs for the beneficiaries.

He tells the story of Jessica, a client who planned to leave her money in the bank to relatives. But her hand-written will used the word "monies," an imprecise term. Jessica's relatives each hired a lawyer and went to court to get a decision. Did monies include her guaranteed investment certificates at the bank? The judge decided it was only cash in her account, but the cost of interpreting the will was high.

Olkovich also talks about Tom, who drafted contracts for a living before he retired. His homemade will said, "I give 10 per cent of my estate to God."

An excellent choice of beneficiaries, said the lawyer who reviewed the will before Tom went on vacation. But which religious organization was to receive the money?

"Between you and God it may be clear, but no one else on earth will know," the lawyer told Tom. "A court would have to interpret your intentions after you're gone."

Olkovich insists he's never seen a do-it-yourself will kit that was filled out correctly. He has practised law since 1978, taught estate planning in Ontario's bar admission course and written a book, *The Complete Idiot's Guide to Wills and Estates for Canadians* (Pearson Education Canada). He even chose the name www.mrwills.com for his Web site.

"The kits say they're lawyer approved," he says. "This means they meet the minimum requirements in each province when they're sold. But no one approves what you do with the kits, how you fill in the blanks."

Lawyers Margaret Kerr and JoAnn Kurtz, authors of *Wills and Estates for Canadians for Dummies* (John Wiley & Sons), are also suspicious of will kits.

"The guides provide only limited advice about planning your will," Kerr and Kurtz argue. "The easy-to-use forms tend to be blank in all of the difficult places and complete only in the places you could probably figure out on your own."

Marketplace, a CBC-TV consumer show, asked the parents of a young child to do their own wills, then took them to lawyer Mary

McGregor to review. The show used the heavily advertised Canadian Legal Will Kit, which McGregor said was too simple and didn't give enough advice or warnings about potential problems.

For example, the will was missing basic information, such as details on how a guardian might raise the daughter, provision for future children and a plan for what would happen to the family's estate if all three died.

A $30 will kit may be a false economy. It's worth paying a lawyer a couple of hundred dollars to prepare a will and save your family a lot of grief later on.

Besides, a professional can help you see the big picture. Planning your estate involves more than writing a will. Sometimes the best thing to do is to pass assets to family members outside your will in order to cut taxes.

How to cut probate taxes

First comes the will. Then comes probate. Then comes probate tax avoidance. This three-step tango is familiar to anyone who has discussed estate planning with a lawyer or financial adviser.

Probate comes from the Latin word for proof. It means proving to a judge that the will is valid and there's no later will.

Suppose your father dies in Ontario, leaving you as his heir and executor in his will. You try to get access to his account, but the bank manager refuses to release the funds without probate.

Banks generally insist on probate because they're trying to protect themselves from liability. What if the bank gives you the money, then someone turns up with another will made by your father? What if your father owed large amounts to creditors? Their claims against his estate would take precedence over your entitlement to the money. What if a new wife materialized, one you didn't know about? Her marriage could revoke your will.

Probate may be unnecessary if the estate is under $5,000. But financial institutions holding estate assets generally want the court's seal of approval on the most recent valid will.

Even if your father has no will, his assets still go through probate. The courts appoint an administrator to handle the estate.

Many people try to avoid probate. A complete description of the estate's contents must be filed with the court, becoming a matter of public record. This can be embarrassing.

Further, lawyers are usually involved. You can probate an estate yourself, but this requires a lot of detail work and may result in delays in distributing the estate.

Provincial probate tax is also levied on the estate's value. Ontario's tax is $15 for each $1,000 of estate value, the highest in Canada, amounting to $7,000 on a $500,000 estate and $14,500 on a $1 million estate. Other provinces have raised their rates too.

You can reduce probate costs by designating a beneficiary other than your estate for your RRSP. You can also hold your home jointly with right of survivorship. This avoids probate if one of the owners survives.

But while probate-tax avoidance is a popular sport, the solutions are often extreme and can endanger a family's financial health. Barry Corbin, an estate planning lawyer in Toronto, has identified the potential pitfalls of common strategies:

■ **Putting assets into joint ownership with a spouse.** If one spouse dies, the jointly owned assets pass to the surviving spouse outside the will. But if a husband and wife die together in an accident, probate is still necessary. During a couple's lifetime, jointly owned assets may be exposed to claims against a spouse arising from financial problems. Also, joint ownership means giving up control. One spouse has to get the other spouse's consent before selling the assets or using them as collateral.

■ **Putting assets into joint ownership with a child.** Control is an issue, since jointly owned property cannot be sold or mortgaged without the child's consent. The child's spouse could make a claim for a share of the assets. When a home is involved, the deed has to be reregistered and there may be land transfer tax and capital gains tax arising from the transfer. Also, the parent may lose some of the tax exemption for a principal residence.

■ **Designating a child as beneficiary of a retirement savings plan.** This can cause problems if the child is a minor when the parent dies, since the RRSP proceeds would be paid into court and handed over when the child turns 18. Parents who dispose of assets through a will often set up trusts to make sure children don't inherit everything at once. Part of the money gets paid at age 18 and the rest later.

■ **Transfers of property to a trust**. It's expensive to set up a trust while you are alive. You probably pay more in legal fees than you would to prepare a will. You also face trustee fees and the ongoing responsibility of filing separate trust tax returns. Transfers to a living trust are normally treated as a sale for income tax purposes.

Suppose you own $100,000 worth of shares in BCE Inc. They cost $30,000 when you bought them, so you have a profit of $70,000. If you transfer these shares to a trust, the transfer is treated as a sale for income tax purposes. Half of your $70,000 profit, or $35,000, will be taxable at the capital gains rate.

Stock and mutual fund portfolios and real estate are usually not transferred to a trust, because of the income tax hit that immediately arises. Trusts are used to hold assets that have no built-in gains, such as cash, treasury bills and GICs.

But if you're 65 or older, you can set up a special kind of trust without triggering capital gains tax on the assets at the time of transfer. The tax is deferred and kicks in only when you die or when your spouse dies.

The "alter ego trust" is designed for single people. The "joint spousal trust" is for legally married, common-law or same-sex couples. The goal of these trusts is not to save income tax (since the tax is payable anyway after death), but to minimize or eliminate probate fees. The trust becomes a substitute for a will.

If you or your parents want to set up such a trust, remember there are costs that may outweigh the benefits. You have to prepare a set of trust documents and file a separate income tax return each year.

Remember, too, that the income earned and kept in the trust during your lifetime is taxed at the highest marginal rate. So don't bother to set one up unless you're already in the top tax bracket.

How to cut estate taxes

People often say the United States is a good place to live and Canada is a good place to die. That's because Canada, unlike the United States, does not have an estate tax.

"You might say you're taxed at death in the United States, but you are taxed to death in Canada," say Douglas Gray and John Budd in *The Canadian Guide to Will and Estate Planning* (McGraw-Hill Ryerson).

In 1972, the federal government did away with the estate and gift taxes imposed on the total value of your assets when you die. But at the same time, it introduced a tax on the gains realized when you sell stocks and other investments. These gains used to be tax-free.

The result: You're taxed on the fair market value of your capital assets when you die, whether you sell them or not. Capital assets include stocks, mutual funds, real estate (except for a principal residence) and works of art.

Here's an example. Your father bought $10,000 worth of Royal Bank shares, which had a market value of $40,000 when he died. Canadian tax law handles this as if he had sold those shares on the day of his death. As a result, his estate has to pay capital gains tax on one-half of that $30,000 gain, or $15,000.

There's one exception to this "deemed disposition rule." If your father leaves his Royal Bank shares to a surviving spouse, the tax is deferred until she dies (assuming she doesn't sell them during her lifetime). But the tax kicks in when she passes the shares to other family members either before her death or in her will.

One way to reduce capital gains taxes is to adjust the cost base. This is best understood with a cottage property.

Suppose you and your spouse paid $50,000 for your cottage 10 years ago. Later, you put in $25,000 worth of improvements, such as an extra bedroom and bathroom. The renovations, plus the purchase price, add up to $75,000. That's your adjusted cost base.

If the cottage has a market value of $150,000 when the second spouse dies, the gain is only $75,000—not the $100,000 it would have been if you'd made no improvements.

The capital gains tax payable on death often comes as a surprise. Kids may count on a big inheritance from Mom after Dad dies, only to find the estate is much smaller than they believed it to be.

For most Canadians, the major tax exposure is from investments held in registered retirement savings plans or retirement income plans. If a $100,000 nest egg is taxed at a 30 per cent rate, the estate has to come up with $30,000. This means the investments may have to be sold to pay the taxes, if there's not enough cash in the estate. Sometimes other assets have to be sold, such as the family home, which is supposed to pass to the next generation tax-free.

Here are a few tax-cutting tools that estate planners use:

- **Gifts during your lifetime**. Also known as the "die broke" strategy, making gifts to your loved ones has an added bonus. You can see everyone enjoying the inheritance while you're still around. But while Canada does not tax gifts in the hands of beneficiaries, there may be other taxes to pay. When you give away real estate, antiques, jewelry or art, you're considered to have sold them at fair market value and you have to pay capital gains tax on any increase in value. "If you're giving away assets that will lead to a tax bill, consider giving away those assets slowly, over a number of years, so that you don't trigger a huge tax bill in a single year," says Tim Cestnick in *Winning the Tax Game 2001* (Prentice Hall Canada).

- **Doing an estate freeze.** This involves changing the ownership of an asset, so that the future growth in value is shifted to the next generation. It's a complex planning tactic, commonly used for family businesses and real estate investments. One way to freeze an estate is to transfer assets to a corporation. You take back special shares that are frozen in value and issue common shares (which may appreciate in value over time) to your children. Estate freezing can also work with a trust. However, this is more likely to trigger capital gains tax than transferring assets to a corporation.

- **Leaving assets to your spouse.** You can roll over your estate tax-free by leaving everything to your spouse. By doing so, you will defer capital gains tax until the second spouse dies. If you leave anything to your kids or other heirs, leave them the assets that won't be subject to tax, like cash or a principal residence.

- **Transferring assets to a spousal trust.** This has the same effect as leaving assets directly to a spouse. A trust is a terrific tool for splitting income, says Cestnick. The savings result from the fact that both the spouse and the trust pay low marginal tax rates on the first $30,000 of income.

There's only so much you can do to keep the government's hands off your tax-sheltered retirement savings and other valuable family assets. But you can offset the taxes with life insurance that will pay out tax-free on your death.

You have to ask yourself a few questions before buying life insurance for estate-planning purposes.

"Do your kids really care whether they get more cash after you are dead, or would they prefer to see you live your life more fully with greater cash flow now instead of paying insurance premiums?" asks chartered accountant Kurt Rosentreter in *Rosentreter's Rules: 100 Solutions for Achieving High Net Worth* (Prentice Hall Canada).

"Maybe they are prepared to pay the insurance cost for you. Or maybe they are not. Have a heart-to-heart discussion with the family before you go out and spend a lot of money on an estate-planning insurance policy."

Can you afford the insurance? Suppose your parents are 73 and 75. They have a registered retirement income fund worth $500,000 and they buy a $250,000 life insurance policy to protect half the RRIF's value from taxes. Both spouses are non-smokers and have no life-threatening medical problems.

Cliff Oliver, an actuary and life insurance broker in Toronto, recommends buying term-to-100 universal life, a joint and last-to-die policy that pays out benefits only when the second spouse dies. The best premium rate he found was $6,000 a year, or $500 a month.

Couples can also buy a life insurance policy that is paid up completely after the first spouse dies. It's more expensive, Oliver says, about $10,000 to $11,000 a year.

Life insurance for estate planning is popular with people who have high incomes or own a small business or cottage they've held in the family for years. But remember: This is a non-essential insurance need for most Canadians.

Oliver says he almost never sees adult children buying life insurance policies and paying premiums for their parents. They're too burdened with their mortgages and other financial obligations. "Buying life insurance is a favour you do for your kids," he says.

Don't forget a power of attorney

Writing a will and creating an estate plan are things you do for your loved ones, not for yourself. You hope the arrangements work out well, since you won't be around to see them.

A power of attorney is a financial planning tool that is designed to protect your family while you're still alive. It gives someone else the authority to look after your affairs if you're sick or mentally incapacitated.

The person you pick does not have to be a lawyer. It should be a relative or trusted family friend. It's a good idea to appoint more than one person to act on your behalf. You can designate your spouse and choose someone else to take over if your spouse dies or becomes too ill to continue. Or name two people to act together, so they can police each other.

Talk it over with the people you choose, so you know they're willing to help. And review your choices periodically to make sure the substitute decision-makers can still do the job.

Without a power of attorney, family members can't get on with their lives. They may need a court-appointed trustee to make financial decisions.

Here's what can happen to a young and healthy person struck down by an accident. Lawyer Ed Olkovich tells the story of Stuart, 37, a father of three, who has a serious car accident and is in a coma. As his condition gradually improves, his wife Lilly considers refinancing their home or selling it and moving closer to his rehabilitation clinic. Lilly approaches the family lawyer and finds, to her horror, that the house was registered in both their names. She can't sell or refinance it unless she gets permission from a court.

"Stuart and I prepared wills. Won't that help?" Lilly asks the lawyer. No, the lawyer replies. Stuart's will is not effective until after his death. The couple should have prepared a power of attorney for property.

Now, Lilly has to apply through the courts to get the relief she needs. This can mean hiring a lawyer and providing assessments from professionals that Stuart is unable to manage his property. And once the court appoints a trustee to take over Stuart's finances, the court will have to supervise and audit the trustee's activities.

"Surprised and stunned. That's the reaction people have when we review these incapacity laws," Olkovich says.

In Ontario, families can hire a qualified assessor, usually a social worker, who follows specific guidelines set down by the Public Guardian and Trustee. Assessors charge $50 to $150 an hour and take four to six hours to do a financial guardianship. The total cost is less than $1,000. For information, call 416-327-6683 or 1-800-366-0335.

A power of attorney is relatively inexpensive. Lawyers' fees are in the $100 range and do-it-yourself kits cut the cost in half. But pre-printed forms may not cover your individual needs.

There are ways to prevent misuse. Your lawyer can hold the document for you and require an independent expert opinion before it can be activated. You also can require annual financial statements from the trustee or oversight by an accountant.

Most people, of course, manage their finances until they die and won't need to use a power of attorney. The document is there as an insurance policy, to protect you from a possible disaster.

A continuing power of attorney is not to be confused with a more limited power of attorney you give to someone to act on your behalf if you're out of town for long periods. Financial institutions usually ask you to sign their own POA forms, regardless of any other documents you have prepared.

In Ontario, you can get a legally binding power of attorney from the Office of the Public Guardian and Trustee, part of the Ministry of the Attorney-General. It's the substitute decision-maker of last resort, which steps in when no one is available to act on behalf of an incapacitated person.

Write to the Public Guardian and Trustee, 595 Bay St., Suite 800, Toronto, Ont., M5G 2M6, or call 416-314-2800 or 1-800-366-0335. Kits are also available from MPPs, local libraries and on the Internet. (Go to www.attorneygeneral.jus.gov.on.ca and click "How May We Help You?" and then "Protecting Vulnerable Persons.")

When doing your power of attorney, here are some things you should know:

- You must be 18 or older and mentally capable, which means you know what property you have and its value and what authority your attorney will have.

- You can choose anyone you want, as long as he or she is 18 or older. Many trust companies are prepared to act as an attorney and charge a fee for this service.

- You can name more than one person but the law will require them to make decisions together unless you specifically give them permission to act separately. If you let your attorneys make decisions together, it's a good idea to specify how disagreements get resolved.

- Your attorney is compensated at a rate set out in provincial law, unless you say otherwise.

- You must sign the forms in front of two witnesses, who are there together.

- You can revoke the power of attorney at any time, as long as you write it down on paper and sign again in front of two witnesses.

- Both a husband and wife should have their own continuing powers of attorney for property. One document won't work for two spouses.

In most provinces, you can also appoint someone to step in and make medical decisions for you if you can't act for yourself. This is known as a power of attorney for personal care. It's a separate document from a power of attorney for property, though some provinces allow the two to be combined into one.

Read a good estate planning book

Just five years ago, you couldn't find a single book for average Canadians on estate planning. Today, there's a wealth of choices, including the one that started the mini-publishing boom. Sandra Foster's *You Can't Take It with You: The Common-Sense Guide to Estate Planning for Canadians* has sold more than 100,000 copies.

Publisher John Wiley & Sons has just come out with a fourth edition of Foster's book, a 320-page paperback that's packed with tips, examples and Q&A nuggets. There's also a hands-on companion, *The Estate Planning Workbook*.

Behind the success of these books is a demographic trend. Boomers in their 40s and 50s are looking after elderly parents and contemplating their own mortality. "As they get involved in doing an estate plan for their parents, they think about one for themselves, too," says Jamie Golombek, vice-president of tax and estate planning at AIM Funds Management.

Here are a few books that have come out since Foster's bestseller, appealing to different niche markets. Some are more technical and others are easier to understand:

The Complete Idiot's Guide to Estate Planning in Six Simple Steps for Canadians, by Edward Olkovich (Pearson Education Canada).

Wills and Estate for Canadians for Dummies, by Margaret Kerr and JoAnn Kurtz (John Wiley & Sons).

Despite the off-putting titles, I'm a fan of these books. Their approach makes even the most arcane topics intelligible to those who don't normally follow them, using funny titles and drawings. I prefer the Kerr-Kurtz guide, which is organized better and easier to skim through to find information. (They put all the stuff about trusts into one chapter, for example, while Olkovich scatters it around.) Also, they include more on basic financial planning.

Everything You Need to Know About Estate Planning, by Kevin Wark (Key Porter).

Wark, a tax lawyer and president of Equinox Financial Group, takes more of a financial-planning approach. He devotes a chapter to business owners, which some books don't touch. This is definitely a light read, with just over 200 pages. It's intended to give you just enough information so you can go to an expert (presumably someone like Wark) to draft your estate plan.

The Canadian Guide to Will and Estate Planning, by Douglas Gray and John Budd (McGraw-Hill Ryerson).

Gray is a lawyer and Budd is a chartered accountant. Put them together and you get a book that's weighty and thorough and just a bit dull. It's 360 pages but feels longer. Now in its second edition, the book has added a couple of chapters (on selecting a retirement home and planning your funeral). There's also a related Web site, www.estateplanning.ca. If you're a serious person and a detail freak, you'll want this book on your shelf. Case studies add some human interest, but you'll find not a smidgen of levity, just the facts.

The Family Fight: Planning to Avoid It, by Barry Fish and Les Kotzer (Continental Atlantic Publications).

Fish and Kotzer, both estate planning lawyers in Toronto, have seen how families can be torn apart when someone doesn't plan properly for death or disability. In their book and Web site, www.family-fight.com, they tell stories meant to scare you into doing something and sharing information on what you've done with your significant others. They say a culture of secrecy and lack of communication makes even the best estate plans go awry. Their book, a slim 136 pages, could use an index. Don't miss the chapter called "Inheriting Turmoil—Real Life Examples."

I Am the Executor: What Do I Do? by David J.C. Nicholl (Nimbus Publishing).

The title says it all. Many people say yes when a close friend or relative asks them to be an executor of a will, without knowing what responsibilities they are taking on. Eventually they'll be dealing with a mess of legal documents, financial issues and government agencies or courts. Nicholl, a retired banker, is a financial and estate consultant living in Halifax. He binds his narrative together with a fictional case study of a widow who has to administer her husband's estate after his sudden death. This 144-page, large-format book, published in 1999, is hard to find in stores. You can order it online from www.chapters.indigo.ca or get it directly from Nimbus Publishing Ltd., P.O. Box 9301, Station A, Halifax, N.S. B3K 5N5; phone (902) 455-4286.

Food for Thought: Bringing Estate Planning to Life, by Jean Blacklock, Judy Miyashiro and Susan Murphy (John Wiley & Sons).

I've saved the most delicious book for last. The authors (a banker, a chef and a writer) tell the story of seven imaginary friends who meet every few months for an elegant meal while they discuss common estate planning dilemmas. You'll find lots of sweet desserts here (along with savoury starters and main courses). The recipes eat up a chunk of the

224-page text and get a separate index at the back. This is a book for those who find it easier to digest a few financial morsels if they're dispensed with dinner. It's a good introduction to the subject.

Now get going!

I procrastinate, you procrastinate, we procrastinate. It's part of human nature to wait until the last minute to get tedious things done. That's why so many people line up at banks in the last week of February to make their RRSP contributions, and why they rush to the post office at midnight on April 30 to mail their tax returns.

Deadlines are great because they focus the mind. Unfortunately, there's no drop-dead date to organize your personal finances. You can go forever without switching banks or insurance companies to get a better deal. You can keep using a high-interest credit card, even though you don't pay off the balance each month, and never get around to applying for a low-interest card. You can stick with the same financial adviser and the same investments, knowing they're unsuitable but not wanting to shake things up.

You can also wait too long to get your paperwork in order. You may know where you keep all your documents and records, but have you told your family? Have you put together a list of names and numbers for emergency purposes? You can't predict when you might have to hand over your finances to someone else. Get your act together now.

Now get going!

Money 101 isn't an easy course. Many of us fail the first time and have to try again. The key is to take small steps. Work on your spending first, then your saving. Tame the credit monster before putting together a retirement plan. Don't let your investments exceed your comfort zone. Do some estate planning and put aside money for your children's post-secondary education.

Getting financially fit is similar to getting physically fit. At first, the least amount of exertion tires you out. You run five minutes and you're out of breath. The next day, your muscles are stiff and your bones ache. You can't imagine how you'll ever get to your goal of running a 10-kilometre race.

But if you don't give up, you find yourself getting stronger. Soon you can run 10 minutes before stopping. The stiffness and aches go away. You have more energy, your clothes fit better and your mind is free to wander and problem-solve in a way that doesn't happen when you're sitting down. You love what running does for you, even if you don't enjoy the hard work.

Eventually, running becomes a part of your routine, a habit you can't break. You have achieved a level of fitness you know will improve your health and maybe extend your life. You don't want to give it up and go back to the sedentary existence you had before. And you sure don't want to buy a wardrobe of bigger clothes.

Starting a financial fitness regimen is also a strain. You miss the things your money doesn't buy when you cut back your spending. It hurts to put an extra $25 a month into savings or debt reduction if you have to deprive yourself of something that makes life more fun— going to the movies, eating out, buying new gadgets for the home.

So you grumble and you feel pained and you're tempted to give up. But soon you start to see results. Your savings multiply and turn into a tidy sum of money, which makes you feel more secure about the future. Your credit card balances start to dwindle and you can count the months until they're paid off. You feel confident you have the resources to cope with whatever life throws at you.

Financial fitness, like physical fitness, becomes a habit if you keep going long enough. When you get used to living on $25 a month less than before, you can crank up your savings to $50 a month and see how that feels. Soon there are tangible results and you're more motivated to continue, less tempted to backslide. You don't want to lose the momentum and start all over again.

Just as athletes do better with coaching, you may do better if you have a money coach. A good financial adviser will help you measure your progress and stay on track. Keep looking for someone you trust and don't settle for someone who's not the right fit.

Not everyone needs professional assistance. Some people are uncomfortable discussing their finances with an outsider. It's okay if you prefer doing things yourself. But your spouse and family should know the game plan and lend their support. Don't shut them out.

My final advice: Don't be overly ambitious. If you take on too many jobs at once, you're more likely to fail. Pick just one thing in your financial life you want to improve and stick with it until you see some results. Then, move on to the next job you want to tackle.

Becoming financially fit is hard work. Let's not kid ourselves. You can scrimp and save for years and still not achieve what you want. But doing something is better than doing nothing. You'll be better off even if you get only part of the way toward your goal.

It's the journey that counts, not the destination. I wish you all a smooth and safe trip.

Index

Index

Index

Consumer Federation of America,
36–37
Consumer Reports magazine, 52, 53, 73
Consumer's Guide to Insurance, 48
Convenience Consumer, 15
convertible bonds, 187
Corbin, Barry, 256
Cordeiro, Mary, 206
core and explore, 200
cost-cutting, how to, 9
Costello, Brian, 157
cost of living, calculating, 7
coupon, 185
credit cards, 11, 82–98
"Credit Cards and You," 87
Credit Counselling Service of Toronto, 7
credit
  rating, 96–98
  repair services, 102
  report, 99–102
credit union, 20–22
  and reverse mortgage line of credit, 146
  insurance, 28
Credit Union Central of Canada, 21, 28
Croft, Richard
  Investing Strategies 2001, 205

debit card, 23–25
debt
  eliminating, 109–10
  transferring, 11
Debt-Free Graduate, 231
deemed disposition rule, 259
deferred sales charges (DCS), 196
den Ouden, Marco
  The 50 Best Science and Technology Stocks for Canadians, 208
deposit insurance, 28
DesRosiers, Dennis, 76
disability, defined, 35
disability insurance, 34–35
discretionary money manager, 153
dividend
  reinvestment plan (DRIP), 171–72
  stock, defined, 176

yield, 176
divorce, and financial planning, 239–42
do-it-yourself will kit, 251
dollar cost averaging (autopilot investing), 168–70, 171, 172
Dranoff, Linda Silver, 240, 241
  Everyone's Guide to the Law, 239
DRIP (dividend reinvestment plan), 171–72
Dutka, Randy, 118

economic indicators, Web sites for, 208
Edmonston, Phil
  Lemon-Aid, 52–53, 73
education, saving for, 214–31
eight-step formula, for child support, 243–44
emergencies, paying for, 32–33
Employment Insurance, 34
Ennis, Dale, 172
Equifax Canada Inc, 100
equity fund, 193
estate planning books, 266–69
Estate Planning Workbook, 266
estate taxes, and financial planning, 258–61
Everyone's Guide to the Law, 239
Everything You Need to Know About Estate Planning, 267
exchange-traded fund (ETF), 200
extended warranties, 52–53

Family Fight: Planning to Avoid It, 268
family plan for RESP, 221
family trust, 227
financial advisers, 148–55
Financial Consumer Agency of Canada
  and high interest, 88
  and interest-free period, 92
  and late payments, 90
  "Credit Cards and You," 87
  Web site, 28
Financial Planners Standards Council of Canada, 150, 152
Financial Services Commission of

Index

Index

Index

Index